Born a Burden: A Story of an American Orphan is published under Voyage books, sectionalized division under Di Angelo Publications INC.

VOYAGE BOOKS

an imprint of Di Angelo Publications. Born a Burden: A Story of an American Orphan Copyright 2018 Jim Fiume in digital and print distribution in the United States of America.

Library of congress cataloging-in-publications data

Born a Burden: A Story of an American Orphan   Downloadable   via   Kindle, iBooks   and NOOK.

Library of Congress Registration

Hardback

ISBN-10: 1-942549-37-7

ISBN-13: 978-1-942549-37-6

Developmental Editor: Elizabeth Geeslin

Cover Design: Savina Deianova

1. Non-fiction

2. Non-fiction ——Biography ——Memoir—— United States of America with

int.   distribution

Born a Burden
a Story of an American Orphan

Jim Fiume

Table of Contents

Dedication

This book is for anyone who was raised in an orphanage or in the foster care system, and for anyone who has ever been orphaned and abandoned by their family. It's for anyone who ended up on the streets like I did—and for those people who feel that life will never get any better. It will if you believe that something better will come along and keep looking for it.

I dedicate this book to my brother, who, unlike me, gave up on life.

"There is no education like adversity."
- Benjamin Disraeli

Born Abandoned

Chapter 1

"Jim! Get out of that god-damned tree now!" my grandmother screamed in broken Italian. I was halfway up one of her cherry trees that she used to harvest cherries for moonshine. She came outside after me, raging like a bull, yanking me out of the tree onto the ground. Without offering me a hand to pick me up, she continued back into the house, mumbling in Italian under her breath. I don't know what she was saying, but I could feel the intention. I moved on to find something else to do, out of her sight. Like most kids, I needed to move, to be in action. I was a bit hyper, but I wasn't any different than most little boys under the age of 5.

My grandmother yelled at me a lot, which seems like a normal thing for Italian grandmothers to do if you go by what you see in the movies. But this was different. Her yelling at me came from a place of regret and loathing. There was something deep within it that bellowed how much she wished things were just different. It wasn't that she hated me, but everything she did and said made it pretty clear that she regretted having me around.

It was like that most of the time for me. "Dammit, Jim, get out of that! Jim! Stop touching those! Sit down! Stop it dammit!" I might have thought my name was Dammit had I not known any better.

I didn't know better about a lot of things growing up. I didn't know it wasn't normal to get the crap smacked out of me for the smallest bit of mischief. I didn't know that there were some kids who never had to cope with being tossed from one home to another, not knowing who their mother was or what it felt like to have a stable home. I didn't know it wasn't normal to never be hugged. My normal was being screamed at, pushed around and abandoned over and over again without any real clue as to why it was happening or when it would stop.

I didn't even know that I was in a situation that a lot of people today would look at and say, "Wow, Jim, you had it pretty rough." Some people had it a lot rougher, and I can appreciate that, but it didn't take away from the fact that I was given away three times. The only thing I knew for sure growing up was that each day was a new day, and that each day, whether I was five or fifteen, I would wake up and make the best out of it, even if that meant living in the back of a grocery store because I needed a place to stay, and keeping the floor clean in exchange for the sleeping space—which, believe me, is a good offer and one I took more than once.

My brother Frankie and I were a part of the system, abandoned and tossed from family to orphanage to foster care in the span of our first 11 years. Every person handles that sort of thing differently. We tell ourselves things to make ourselves feel better. While I was telling myself that each day was a new day and I knew that I had something better coming to me, my brother, Frankie, didn't have that same inner dialogue. Although we started out much the same, we ended up on opposite sides of the spectrum with regard to our views toward our life and its purpose.

I was born in 1948, at St. Mary's Maternity Hospital and Children's Home in Lyncourt, New York, just outside of Syracuse. The hospital was known, at that time, for taking care of unwed mothers. It was also a place in which mothers could leave or abandon a child that they could not take care of. In my case, so I was told, I had both a mother and father who abandoned me. So, I remained in the hospital with other babies being taken care of by the nuns. Supposedly my father's mother, my grandmother, was the only one who came to visit me. I was too young to remember.

The only memory I have of the place was being placed in tube, sliding down a long way and being taken out by the nuns at the bottom. Somehow, I've rememb-

12

ered that story for nearly 70 years, and I was not even two years old at the time. I returned many years later to find that the hospital is still there, but it is no longer a place for abandoned children. And there, on the side of the building, was the long tube which was used for getting babies and young children out of the building safely in the event of a fire. As it turns out, there was a fire while I was there as a very small child. I smiled when I saw it, because now I knew for sure it wasn't something I imagined.

As I got a little older, I learned a lot about my family. Apparently, my grandmother and grandfather immigrated to America from the southern part of Italy back in 1929. Like so many immigrants, they made their way by boat to Ellis Island. They settled on the Lower East Side of Manhattan with thousands of immigrants from all over the world. It was an overcrowded working-class neighborhood, but the people coming to the United States were just happy to be in a country with so many possibilities. I have no idea how long they stayed in New York City, or how they got to Syracuse, but that's where they ended up. They had four children—two boys, Frank, who was my father, and my uncle Paul. There were also two daughters, my aunts Rose and Jeannette.

My father was never really much of a "father", so to speak. He was just one of those uneducated guys who got married and, due to the circumstances in which he found himself, happened to have kids. Instead of working, he was into gambling, drinking and acting like a tough guy. In his mind, he thought that was work. He was basically a gangster wannabe. He married my mother, Virginia Caruso, whom I never met, when they were both pretty young.

I was told that they had a daughter that died of pneumonia because he had no money to pay the heating bill. They then had my brother in 1946 and two years, in 1948, I came along.

For some reason unbeknownst to me, maybe to make him sound important or glorify him in some way, my aunts, Rose and Jeannette used to tell me that my dad worked for the CIA. Once I got to know my dad, I knew that he didn't have the education to work for the CIA. In fact, he probably couldn't even spell CIA. But I remember when they first told me about the CIA, I couldn't stop laughing. Maybe it was meant to be a joke, since you have to be educated, ethical and sober to work for an intelligence organization, and he was not any of those things.

As for my Uncle Paul, he was the most likable of the whole bunch of them. He was a happy, fun loving wino who didn't have a mean bone in his body. He was always jolly and laughing about something. Paul was the kind of guy you never had to worry about saying the wrong thing around. He kept things lighthearted and he didn't seem to have a care in the world. He was the nicest person anyone could meet—and because of these attributes, probably one of the reasons everyone else in the family seemed to treat my brother and I so coldly. By comparison to Uncle Paul, just about any other attitude was cold.

That was the family, and the one thing they all had in common was that none of them had any vested interest in my brother or me. What I would later learn was that real "family" does not have to be blood relatives. I found this out at the age of two when I was lucky enough to become part of a terrific family.

Since we were Italian, my brother and I were taken from the orphanage into the home of an Italian couple, Carmella and Joseph Grande—two of the nicest people anyone could hope to meet. They were going to adopt us, raise us, and give us a good home. At last, after my long stay in the hospital of unwanted children, I was going to have a real life.

The Grandes had apparently visited me often in the hospital, and I was told that they were going to be my mother and father. I was very young, so I probably didn't know what that truly meant. Most babies are held by their mothers as infants, so they know who their mothers are. Even though they can't understand what that means, babies that are only a few months old can recognize the face and voice of their mothers. I had no idea what that was like, so when Carmella Grande would visit me and pick me up, I must have thought it was terrific. I didn't know any differently. As for my brother, he knew our parents. He was with them for two years, so he was a lot more confused and screwed up when he suddenly went from living with mom and dad to the Grande's home, who he had to accept as his new mom and dad.

The Grandes lived in Liverpool, New York, about six miles away from Syracuse. They had a nice house, although it was small, maybe 1,200 square feet. There were two bedrooms, a kitchen, living room, and bathroom. In the house right behind, theirs was Carmella's sister and her family. They also had a nice house and we would go back and forth along a path to and from their house. I felt like I was part of one big family. This had become my home and I was a happy little boy.

Joseph Grande, who I called dad, worked at a washing machine manufacturer that made the old-fashioned machines. These were the ones where you'd put the cloth through a wringer and it went from one tub to the other and then into a pool of clear water. The company was called Easy Washer and, at the time, their machines were quite innovative. Meanwhile, Carmella, my mom, stayed home and took care of my brother and me. I was one happy kid. I became friends with the kid across the street—we played all sorts of games and ran wild in the backyard. It was a good life for a little kid.

I remember proudly walking to school with my mom. I was going to kindergarten and my brother was in second grade. I also remember when I'd get home from school, there would always be snacks waiting on the table. I made a lot of friends in school, but my brother did not. He spent a lot of time in his room. We usually got along just fine, but there was one time when I stuck something sharp in his ear. I don't remember if I was mad at him or just trying to be annoying, but his ear started bleeding and my dad, Joe, got very mad at me. But it didn't last long—Joe knew how to be a father. He may have been mad and I got in trouble, but it was part of being a kid. The Grandes liked having us in their home, and we were glad to be there.

We were well fed, had clean clothes to wear to school every day and most importantly, we had parents who loved us. It was, in hindsight, the only time in my life, until many years later, that I ever really felt loved. There was a point when I was about six years old when the Grandes packed up and took off for Brooklyn, taking my brother and me with them. We went to stay at a relative's house. Since Joe could not quit his job, he would drive to Brooklyn and join us on weekends. Brooklyn was a totally different world compared to Liverpool. It was 1954, and there I was, a kid from a small suburb of Syracuse now in the middle of a very crowded borough of New York City.

We settled in the Canarsie section of Brooklyn where Carmella's cousin was living with her new husband. Canarsie, which sat along Jamaica Bay, was home to mostly working-class Italian and Jewish immigrant families at that time. I knew very little about baseball, but everyone in Brooklyn constantly talked about their beloved Dodgers, who usually lost the World Series to the Yankees. Little did they know at the time, but the Dodgers would finally beat the Yankees a year later, in the 1955 series, and then leave Brooklyn for good three years later. And little did I know that I would become a huge Yankees fan (still am).

All of the houses in Canarsie had a similar look and were probably built around the same time, early 1900s. They were tenement houses built very close together with little room on either side. They all had stairs in front going down to the sidewalk. But inside, each one had just enough room for a family and there were families in everyone. Some had three generations of family living on three levels, under one roof. Every day at 5 o'clock everyone would come outside and sit on the steps visiting each other, all talking in a mixture of Italian and English.

Italians could talk like you've never heard in your life—very animated, with plenty of hand gestures. Some would scream and yell, others would whisper, probably about their neighbors. Men would play guitars and sing while the neighbors joining in. It was a jovial atmosphere, kind of like an endless street fair. There were also other kids around my age and we would play, but we had to stay near our parents, and as far as I knew, the Grandes were my parents.

While we were all outside, the vegetable man would come down the street selling fresh vegetables from the back of his horse drawn wagon. Obviously, I knew nothing about business at that age, but looking back, that guy was making a bundle as Italian mothers who loved to cook would surround him, buying everything he had. There was also a guy who would come by each morning and put out bottles of milk on the stoops. The cream would be on top of the milk where the neck of the bottle was, and I remember opening them up and stealing some cream. But my favorite salesman was the Italian ice guy. For a nickel, you could get a cup of ices with a wooden spoon. I loved those ices.

My brother continued to spend much of his time in his room, but we both went to a local school for the five or six months that we were living there. The school was a lot larger than the one in Liverpool—a big old red brick building—but inside the kids, at that age, were pretty much the same as those in Liverpool, except I guess they were mostly Italian. At six years old, we just liked to run around and play; we didn't have a care in the world.

On the weekends, we'd go to Coney Island where I got to go on some of the rides. If it was up to me, I would have gone on all of them, but some had age and height requirements. I was a wild kid, sometimes out of control and even becoming a wise guy...but I was really happy. My brother...not so much. He would go on some of the rides, but also sit with our parents and just watch me a lot of the time. He was unusually quiet for an eight year old kid. Looking back, he needed someone to talk to so he could get some professional help, but nobody knew that at the time.

Before we'd leave Coney Island, we'd stop at Nathan's. This was the original Nathan's Restaurant that became world famous for their hot dogs...and the fries were pretty good, too. They opened back in 1916, with ten cent hot dogs, and then they lowered the price to five cents. When we were there, in 1954, I think the price was about twenty cents. Today, after 100 years in business, Nathan's is still there, selling their famous hot dogs for $3.99.

Later that the summer, we abruptly packed up headed back to Liverpool, as quickly as we had arrived. I had no idea why we were in Brooklyn for those months, but I would later learn that it was to get away from our grandmother.

Apparently, she had been giving the Grandes a hard time about raising us and thought we should be with our own family. To learn her opinion about us being raised by the Grandes was a little odd, because she had never expressed any interest in us over the years—why, all of the sudden, was she interested in having my brother and me living with her and my grandfather?

It wasn't too long after we had returned to Liverpool from Brooklyn that my grandmother started coming around to visit. She was suddenly getting involved in our lives. One particularly odd afternoon, there was a huge fight between the Grandes and my grandmother. They were yelling at each other and my dad, Joe Grande, kept telling her to leave. But my grandmother was as stubborn as they come. She would not go unless my brother and I came with her. Next thing I knew, Frankie and I were leaving the Grande's house with our grandmother. She still had legal guardianship, or some such thing, and would not give it up. The Grandes wanted to finalize the adoption, making it legal and official. It would have been such an easy process. After all, my brother and I had been living there for four years. They knew us and loved us, and we knew them and loved them. That was all that should have mattered. Unfortunately, it did not matter at all to my grandmother.

Why was this happening?

I was later told that the Grandes wanted to legally change our names to Grande, but my grandmother wouldn't let them. I didn't understand why she would she have cared.

I also thought that maybe the Grandes only wanted me and not my brother since he was clearly a troubled kid, but they didn't seem like the kind of people who would think that way. They had treated us both so well.

Then of course, there was the possibility that if my grandmother had us living with her, maybe she could claim us as dependents on her taxes—that was if she actually filed a tax return, which I strongly doubt.

Looking back, none of these answers made much sense. So, why was I ripped from the only people who ever loved me? I had no answer then, and I have no answer now.

I remember yelling that I did not want to go. I kicked and screamed, cried and grabbed at legs and did everything you can imagine a little kid doing in protest. None of it mattered. Both Carmella and Joe gave me a big hug and told me everything was going to be okay. Boy, were they wrong. Everything would never be okay again.

Life in Grandma's World

Chapter 2

I'll never know how or why she did it, but my very own grandmother took me away from the only loving home I ever knew as a child. My life would have been totally different if she had not caused trouble. Who knows how it might have turned out? Would I have become very successful? Maybe. Would I have gone to college? Maybe. Would I have grown up in a loving home? Yes, that I knew for sure.

After the argument, we went back to my grandmother's house. My brother and I were totally confused. I didn't understand why this was happening, but unlike kids today, back in those days kids were not supposed to speak with adults unless spoken to. I remember trying to ask my grandmother when we were going back to the Grande's house, but she was not about to discuss it. She never explained it. All she said was that we were family, she was our grandmother and we were living with her now.

My grandmother's home was in Syracuse, and when we arrived, she showed us where we'd be staying. Her house was complex. It had basically three levels to it. There was a basement where she kept her animals pinned up for slaughter, and there was a lower level kitchen for butchering meat and cooking large meals. On the next level up, which was more of a ground level, there was a beautiful, immaculately clean kitchen that she used to cook but more as a serving kitchen.

There was a dining room and living room, and there were a couple of spare rooms. Upstairs were the regular, nice bedrooms of the home. My grandmother had me and my brother stay in one of the small rooms on the first level—one step up from the basement.

We would soon learn that unlike other sweet little old grandmothers, our grandma was a bootlegger, making and selling illegal bottles of wine. As we would find out years later, my Aunt Rose told me she was connected with Joe Kennedy, the patriarch of the Kennedy family, who was known to have had "mob connections". I have no idea if she also had any mobster buddies, but I wouldn't bet against it. What I did know was that she had two houses, one in which she and my grandfather were living, and one in the back where she made gallons of wine. I wasn't supposed to go into that house, but of course I did. I tasted the wine and didn't like it, but most six-year old kids don't have a taste for wine. I preferred grape juice.

For the next eight or nine months, my brother and I remained with our grandparents. We were really only living with our grandmother since my grandfather spent almost all his time sitting at home drinking wine. Grandma made it and he drank it. He rarely ever spoke to us or even acknowledged that we were in the house. He really didn't do much of anything. In fact, the only exercise he ever got was when he ran out of wine and walked to the other house to get some more. Looking back, he probably drank half of my grandmother's potential profits.

My aunt Jeanette was also living there. She was about fifteen at the time, and babysat for us when everyone else was out. I don't think she liked having to babysit, but she did it anyway. A few times, she'd take me with her when she went to meet her boyfriend. They'd go over to the schoolyard to make out while I played on the swings or went down the slide or did pretty much anything I wanted to do. Schoolyards were popular hangouts in those days. I'm not sure where my brother was on those nights. They probably just left him alone in his room—he was almost nine, so he could entertain himself by reading or playing alone.

I remember telling my grandmother about Jeanette and her boyfriend making out. Jeanette would get yelled at and then she'd chase me around trying to hit me with a hairbrush, but she couldn't catch me. Being little and thin has its advantages...I was very fast.

Sometimes, being a typical boy, I would also sneak a peek at her when she was changing her clothes—she never caught me. I wasn't doing it to be weird, just to do something I knew I wasn't supposed to do. Like I said, I was a mischievous little kid. My Aunt Rose, grandma's other daughter, had already grown up, gotten married and moved out, so I wasn't able to torment her like Aunt Jeanette.

Every once in a while, my father would show up from seemingly nowhere and stay in the house. He would drop in at any hour day or night, coming back from somewhere, quite possibly jail. The first time he showed up, my grandmother introduced him to my brother and me as our father, which was hard for me to understand at six years old, because Joseph Grande was my father. I'm sure my brother recognized him and probably understood everything a lot more than I did— he was probably very upset inside. This was the father who had dumped him. We never ever saw our mom. She had run off and nobody knew where she went. Frankie had known her as young child, so that had to be very painful for him as well.

What made it so strange was that this man, our biological "father", showed absolutely no interest in us. He was always running off somewhere. The only real difference between him and my mother was that he would reemerge occasionally, but not for any altruistic reason. My grandmother would ask him in Italian where he was going, but he wouldn't respond. She probably had a good idea what he was up to—she wasn't oblivious to things. After all, she knew the kids he grew up with. He had hung out with a lot of tough Italian kids, and back in those days, my father was hanging around with Italians who got into a lot of trouble. They were gamblers, bootleggers (like my grandmother) or running all kinds of illegal operations. Some might have been connected to the mob, others were gangster wannabes. Yet, if they knew the right people, they could stay out of trouble. That may also have been why my father would sometimes stay at my grandmother's house. If the cops were closing in on him for gambling or whatever crap he was up to, he knew he'd be safe there.

All I knew was that no matter what he was up to, he didn't have time for me or Frankie. One day, I remember my grandmother yelling at him to get us out of the house. "Take these kids to the movies," she yelled in a mixture of broken English and Italian. I was probably driving her to the verge of madness, so she just needed us out of the way. So, my dad took us to see the movie The Day the Earth Stood Still. The movies cost a quarter back then. When we got back to the house, he immediately took off somewhere. There was no "goodbye", no "see you tomorrow"; we never knew if, or when, we'd see him again.

Looking back, life wasn't all that bad at grandma's. I think I was just extra resentful to be there because I had been pried away from the Grande's nice home. I went to first grade at Lemoyne Grammar School on Lemoyne Avenue. I was the new kid in the neighborhood, but I seemed to fit in just fine. I made some friends and Grandma even let some of them come over to play in the backyard, as long as we didn't bother her or break anything. I also looked forward to the weekends, when I'd go food shopping with Grandma at the local market. This was not your typical food shopping trip. My grandmother grew up in the farmlands of Italy in the 1920s. Her family was very poor, so going out to get food meant getting a hold of some animals and killing whatever you were going to eat. Because of her upbringing, Grandma, who had plenty of money from her bootlegging business and a brand-new refrigerator, still went out and bought live animals to kill and cook.

As I mentioned, she kept them in a basement area under the cellar stairs she had a big pen with roosters, chickens, ducks, sometimes even a goat. When it was time for dinner, she'd kill one of them and cook it. It seemed old-school to everyone at the time, but in reality, it was the best way to eat. The meat was fresh, and my grandmother didn't hesitate to cook a huge, traditional old-world meal. At the time, people were slowly transitioning into the typical American lifestyle where everything was becoming prepackaged and convenient.

Even though the animals were there to be our food, I remember letting all them all out so they would run all over the cellar, shitting all over the place. For me they were like pets to play with and each week we'd get new ones. It was great for me so long as I didn't get too attached to one, which I never did. She also had a dog, not to eat, but as a real pet. I played with him a lot.

Oddly enough, on one hand she was killing her own food, like she did in the old country; but on the other hand, she had all sorts of modern conveniences. Besides the refrigerator, she had a modern washing machine, the latest vacuum cleaner and a brand new television set. Many people did not yet have television in the 1950s, but she did. It was one of those large floor model sets, black and white of course, since color TV didn't come around until the 1960s. When I look back, I think about how good we had it at grandma's, but without any love it never felt like we had it good. If I could have somehow magically combined the Grande's love with my grandma's home, it would have been amazing.

Since I never really wanted to go to sleep (I had way too much energy), I would often leave my room and quietly knock on the door to the living room where my grandmother would watch TV. My brother and I had to stay in the rooms on that floor, close to the entrance to the basement with the animals, so I could hear when Grandma was still up watching TV and hadn't gone upstairs to where the regular bedrooms were to go to sleep.

We had beds in the room Grandma gave us and it wasn't all that bad, except for the smell of the animals from the cellar. She and my grandfather, as well as Jeannette, had bedrooms on the second floor. Rose also had a bedroom on the third floor, which stayed empty since she had moved out and for whatever reason, Grandma wouldn't give me and Frankie that room.

On those nights when I'd walk into the living room, my grandmother would invite me to come in and watch television with her. We'd watch Jack Benny, The

Arthur Godfrey show, The Art Linkletter Show, Sing Along with Mitch, The Ed Sullivan Show, Milton Berle, Red Skelton, Lawrence Welk, Perry Como, all sorts of popular shows at the time. These were all shows that grownups watched—there wasn't much programming for kids back then—but I just liked being able to watch TV.

The overall tone at my grandmother's house, the one that would just make my skin crawl, was that no one seemed to love anyone. My grandma didn't seem to love my grandpa, and she sure didn't show love toward her sons. My aunts didn't show love to us, therefore it was just a cycle of coldness passed to each of us by each other over and over again on a daily basis. Nobody really wanted to be there, regardless of my grandma's modern conveniences. Rose had gotten married and moved out, Jeanette escaped as often as she could to be with her boyfriend, my grandfather had drunk himself into a stupor, my father dropped by only when he needed a place to hide out and my brother spent most of his time alone, sulking. I was the only one who was okay being at Grandma's because I was still only six years old and had no say in the matter. I always thought about the Grandes and wondered what they were doing, and I wondered if my grandmother knew that I would have preferred to have stayed with Joe and Carmella Grande. I also wondered if she realized I still thought of them as my mom and dad.

My brother and I were really second-class citizens at my grandmother's house. Rose's bedroom sat empty the entire time we lived there, perfectly ready for us, yet we had to stay on the main floor, close enough to hear animals—and smell them—constantly. When I watched TV with Grandma, she sat on the couch while I had to sit on a wooden stool. It wasn't a popcorn on the couch type of situation. It was my job to help her bring up the animals for slaughter. We had very few actual toys, so I had to make my own fun, and when she got mad at me, she'd chase me around with a broom. She never caught me though, as I mentioned earlier, I was very fast.

I was always getting into trouble. I was told that I once started a fire in the house, and when they would get deliveries of those big gallons of bleach in the clear bottles, I'd break them. Once, I remember picking all the cherries off of her special cherry tree. She was furious because those were some of the cherries she used to make wine. But she never stayed mad at me for very long. I was a cute little kid, so I could get away with a lot—and I did. It wasn't that I was trying to get into trouble, I just had a lot of energy and a lot of curiosity.

One afternoon, I remember climbing into her new car, a beautiful yellow dodge. She was taking me with her to visit some of her friends, but she wasn't taking Frankie. I was clearly her favorite and I remember her telling her friends, "He gets into everything," and her making them laugh because I was just this cute little kid who liked clowning around.

I'm sure that the special attention I got from grandmother wasn't helping my brother's situation at all. I sometimes tried to get him to come out and play, but most of the time he declined my invitations and stayed to himself.

Being as young as I was, I didn't really understand what in the world his problem was. Here we were, two kids from the same birth parents and so very different. I wanted to run and play and have fun and he always seemed so sad. I still didn't understand exactly why we ended up with our grandmother, but I just went along with it. He was older, and looking back at it, he had already lost two sets of parents. He took it to heart. I didn't. Don't get me wrong, to this day I would have given anything to have had a loving family, but at that time, I guess I was still too young to know what I was missing.

I remember one day, while in the cellar with the animals, I found an opening behind one of the panels in the wall. It led to a small door which let me go outside. I usually had to go upstairs and through the kitchen where Grandma or Jeannette would see me and they always wanted to know where I was going—often they'd tell me I had to stay in because it was too cold or something. But now I had freedom to come and go as I liked. I met a kid with a tree house (not too high up, so we could get into it pretty easily) and we became friends—it was a home away from home. I really liked the idea of freedom, but it did not last long. Apparently one day, I left the little door from the cellar open. Since I always let the animals out of the pen, they also got out of the cellar and into the streets of Syracuse. It was actually very funny as a bunch of chickens, rabbits and a goat ran down the street. But my grandmother wasn't amused. She subsequently padlocked my passage to freedom.

It wasn't long after that incident that my grandmother began packing up the few things my brother and I had. I think she simply could no longer handle me being a completely wild child and she didn't know what to do with my brother. All she told us was to get in the car. I saw my aunt Jeannette looking out her bedroom window as we sat in the backseat of the car. If we were going someplace else, I would have thought Jeannette would be thrilled since she wouldn't have to babysit anymore, but her face was sad. I waved, and she waved back. I didn't know it then, but that would be the last time I'd see her for a very long time.

As the car drove off, I remember thinking, or hoping, that maybe we were going home to the Grandes. That would have made life so wonderful. But that was not where Grandma was taking us. She was taking us to a place that would change our lives forever.

Dumped by my Grandmother

Chapter 3

We pulled up to the front of a massive building at 1654 West Onondaga Street in Syracuse. My grandmother told us we were going inside, but I had no idea why, nor did my brother, but we followed—like lambs going to slaughter.

The building in front of us was an orphanage founded in 1872 for orphaned and homeless boys. Hundreds of boys had lived there by 1955 when my brother and I were ushered into the building. My grandmother talked with several people as my brother and I sat and waited. I asked my brother what this place was, he didn't know, but since we had our stuff with us, he knew we were not going back home.

After what seemed like an eternity, a nun came out and welcomed us to The House of Providence. She smiled at us, introduced herself, and told us to follow her. She headed toward a large and ominous double door. Its presence in front of us was ominous. My brother and I started walking with her toward the door, but my grandmother did not. I turned around and said, "C'mon' Grandma," gesturing for her to follow with us, but she shook her head and shook her head no. This was goodbye, so she hugged us both and left. We did not know what possibly awaited us on the other side of those doors.

The smell was an acidic, sterile smell—the kind that almost burns the nostrils because everything is so overwhelmingly wiped down to prevent illnesses. There were kids everywhere, all boys, mostly black, some Latino and some white. They looked like they were around our ages, some were busy playing, and others stopped to look at us. I started looking around for the cells; I'd seen prison cells in movies. I didn't see any but this looked a lot like a prison. I asked the nun who was walking with us why I was there, what did I do to be put in jail? I thought maybe it was because I let the animals out, or ruined the cherry tree or broke a couple of windows. She told me I didn't do anything wrong.

She continued to lead us around the place, showing us a large cafeteria where we would eat, a playroom and other parts of this massive building. There were so many kids, at least a hundred. She told us about the bus that would take us to and from school every day, and then she showed us where we would sleep. I was relieved to see there were no bars, just beds. My brother and I would be in the same group, even though he was older. Later that day, another nun brought us the few clothes and other stuff our grand-mother had packed for us. I wanted to leave but I didn't even know how I would get out—the place was enormous, and I didn't see a door from where I was now being held captive.

It was an orphanage, I was reassured over and over, but it sure felt like we were in prison. Then we met some of the inmates; this was their territory and they looked at us like we were invading their space. I wanted to tell them that we didn't want to be there any more than they did. But I thought it was best to keep my mouth shut. My brother started to cry, which didn't help matters at all.

There are a lot of orphanage stories, and most of them are true. A lot happens in an orphan home that isn't pleasant. I remember they gave us lockers to keep our stuff. Other kids had many toys in theirs, but we had none. We never had people come and visit us so we never had much of anything to put in those lockers. We were truly forgotten by our grandmother, our father and everyone else. I kept hoping maybe one day she'd come back for us, but each day as people came to visit, I sat there alone. Then I hoped maybe Jeanette would visit or maybe even the Grandes. My brother didn't even expect to see a familiar face, so he didn't bother heading to the place where they allowed visitors. Clearly nobody gave a shit about us. After a while, I stopped going over there as well.

I hadn't been "weaned", not in the way that most children are—not from a mother's breast but weaned in the sense of love and touch and neither had my brother. The kids in the orphanage craved love. The nuns from the House of Providence, which were the original nuns of the orphanage, would give some affection. Some of the kids were desperate for any sort of attention. I remember kids going up to the nuns when the nuns would come around at night to put the cross on their forehead before we went to sleep, grabbing them for a hug—and I realized then that everybody wanted to be hugged. They hadn't been hugged—and everyone needs to be hugged. I wouldn't hug because I didn't want a tough guy to think I was a weak person, even if I wanted to be hugged. I learned the best thing you can ever do in life is realize that if you have a weakness, don't ever show it.

Always act tough, be tough, and people stay away from you. However, this is what I would see every night

—children in desperation for compassion. When you're born and you're pushed aside, and you have no mom and no dad and no one's ever hugged you, you haven't been weaned in the sense that I mean it. I hadn't been hugged—I had a hard time being hugged—I have a hard time to this day. My brother had never been hugged. Most of the kids in this orphanage had never been hugged. The House of Providence nuns would at least make some effort toward us, but the nuns who had escaped the Iron Curtain wouldn't touch us. They didn't speak English and they didn't want anything to do with us.

The nuns ran the whole place, and the other people who worked there had jobs to do, and that was all. So, you can imagine what it felt like. As a kid, you want to be loved by a mom and dad but instead you've got all these mean people there who won't give you the time of day. The Iron Curtain nuns made life even more unbearable. They weren't there when Frankie and I first arrived, but when they came around, it was clear that they weren't there to give any affection. I started to secretly believe that the Hungarian nuns that had escaped the Iron Curtain really weren't nuns; they had used the convent as an excuse to escape and come to America. They were there to keep an eye on us and make sure you stayed in line.

If you didn't listen, you'd get a swift kick in the ass, slap in the face, smack in the back of the head or a swat of a broom on your ass. That's what they did in those days; corporal punishment was completely normal, half the time it wasn't even for doing anything wrong. The thing about dolling out corporal punishment was that getting a swift smack was much quicker and easier than any other type of punishment, so it didn't matter much to me. I'd still carry on and do whatever I wanted to do even if I knew I'd get in trouble because I didn't care about a smack and two seconds of pain. The pain would only last a moment and then I could go on doing whatever it was I wanted.

It was tough being in there with a bunch of sad ass kids. Some were just unfortunate, they had good parents who died in a tragedy, but most of these kids were dropped off by parents who could not, or did not want to, raise them. Some had parents in jail, so they were brought there by the police. Other kids came from horrible neighborhoods—some watched their parents get murdered, in some cases the father shot the mother, or they shot themselves. There were kids of drug addicts or alcoholics. Many of these kids were probably beaten up by their parents. My brother and I had a family out there someplace, two families, if you count the Grandes, but they had no idea where we were.

It was hard on me but even harder on Frankie. He was not a strong boy. I could handle a lot of what we went through, for some reason I just didn't let it get to me. I was small and got picked on a lot, but I just knew I had to take it, including an occasional beating from one of the kids who had to "show me who was boss". I didn't run from anyone, nor did I ever cry. I refused to let them have the satisfaction of knowing they hurt me. And, after a while, they didn't even pick on me —they knew they were stronger physically, but they could not break my spirit. As strange as it may sound, even in that hell hole, I kept thinking that I was special, and not the way that the word is sometimes used today, as in "special education", I just felt that something good (or special) was going to happen in my life. That was a feeling that was innate within me, and a feeling that I never relinquished, regardless of my circumstances.

My brother was the complete opposite in his beliefs. After all he had seen and experienced, he believed that we were white trash. Maybe he was right, but I was not going to go down that road with him. He was not accepted by his peers in a place like this. He was often tormented by kids who thrived on weakness. It was like when a shark smells blood, they attack. I was two years younger, but I tried my best to stick up for him. I remember a couple of Latino kids kicking him and telling him that if he didn't give them his food at lunch that they would kick his ass. I told them to back off. They asked what I was going to do about it. I just told them to get away from him. They did. Instead they went after me. I took a few beatings for my brother, but what else could I do? He was suffering already, beating him up was only going to make it worse. That day, I sat with him at lunch—sometimes I sat with other kids. The two Latino kids had their eye on us, but they knew they'd have to beat me up again before they would get to his lunch. Nothing happened. The nuns were also keeping an eye out for him. They could see how weak he was, but when they weren't around to do anything about it, it sometimes got bad.

While it was bad for Frankie from the start, and it got worse when he realized he was a homosexual. Maybe he knew it all along and perhaps he was quiet and withdrawn because he was struggling with the idea, but an orphanage in Syracuse, full of tough kids, was probably not the best place to let everyone know. Remember, this was the 1950s and being gay was not acceptable. I remember him stealing one of the nun's habits from the laundry room and dressing up in it. At first the other kids thought it was funny, until they realized that he wasn't just goofing around. They started teasing him, poking him and making jokes, but it got worse—I thought they were going to really hurt him, so I swiped some food from kitchen and got the attention of the nuns. They were keeping an eye on me, which meant they were also keeping a closer watch on him. I was very embarrassed by him, but I didn't say anything to anyone. I didn't even know what to say to my brother other than to stop or he was going to get us killed. But it didn't stop him. I was scared that at some point that the other kids might seriously hurt him. Eventually, they just backed off; I can only surmise that they just figured there was something wrong and nothing was going to change that. Being as book smart as he was, it was of no help to him in a place like that. It just stifled everything he had inside of him that could bring him any joy. Like snuffing out a candle, that sort of place snuffed out his happiness entirely.

Meanwhile, during our stay in the prison for unwanted children, we were taken each day by bus to Parochial school. They must have made some sort of arrangement for us to go to that school. The bus would pull up at the school, and we'd attend with kids from the local neighborhood. Of course, coming to school each day in a school bus with writing on the side (in giant letters), that read House of Providence, didn't exactly help us fit in with the other kids. Everybody in the area knew that House of Providence was where all the "troubled" orphan kids came from. The parents of these kids would see us coming and move their kids away from us. In school, I'd be sitting at a desk and other kids would change their seats.

These were kids from loving families, who didn't know what to think of kids like us. The parents didn't want their kids hanging around with us. Some of the parents were just as sheltered and closed minded about us as their own kids. They thought maybe we were all in the orphanage because we were little criminals but too young to go to jail, or maybe because our parents had been horrible criminals and we'd learned to be like them and it was just natural and in our blood.

Regardless of their feelings toward us, a lot of those kids were fascinated by us, especially me, because I was always looking for some excitement. Today, they'd probably say I had ADHD or some such thing, but back then, they just said, "This kid's crazy," but they meant it in a good way, because they knew I loved to clown around and make people laugh.

What the kids in the school didn't know was that deep down inside I felt lower than any of them. I wanted so much to have what they had, a loving family and a nice home. I wished I was them, but I never let them know that. Instead, I acted like nothing bothered me. By not being a chicken shit, or acting weak, they respected me. I never started trouble, but I also didn't back down from anything—and these kids were nowhere as scary as most of the kids at House of Providence. What changed was when the kids started to think I was cool; they began to look up to me.

Then, one day, after school, I slipped out through the playground and took off. I asked my brother to come with me, but he didn't want to, so he got on the bus instead. I saw from down the street that the bus had left and there I was, free. I had made my escape and it was so easy to do. At first, I went and sat on the porch of a really nice house, so the kids that were walking home (that didn't know where I came from) would think I was living there. I can only look back and assume that I didn't have much self-esteem at that time, and making other kids think that I was living a great life in a big house was my way of compensating for what I didn't have.

I had a few hours of being out on my own. In time, the local police caught up with me. They just pulled up in a squad car and asked if I was Jimmy Fiume and I disclosed my true identity. They put me in the back of the police car, and even though they did not handcuff me, I thought I might be going to jail for real. I tried to explain that I didn't do anything.

"I missed the school bus and was trying to walk home, but got lost," was my lame excuse. They didn't say anything. They just took me back to the orphanage.

I guess I was reported missing, so they knew where I belonged. When I got back, I expected to get clobbered by the nuns, but instead they only lectured me on the dangers of running away. Then they sent me back to my group. I figured some of the other kids would start smacking me around or something, but when I told them where I had been, they were impressed that I had the balls to run away. They left me alone.

And so it began. In the six years that I was in captivity at the orphanage, from age seven to thirteen, I must have run away nearly five or six times a year. Sometimes I'd leave from school and other times I'd just slip out of the building when nobody was paying attention. After all, the doors weren't locked. It was an orphanage, not actually a prison, even if it felt like one. Each time, once I was free, I had a sense of street smarts that would allow me to take care of myself in some regard. I never felt in danger or like I was lost. It takes a lot of repressed energy to run away as many times as I did, and I would be remiss to mention that usually a kid doesn't run away without reason. For a long time, I didn't let myself think about the reasons I did anything that I did.

Me (right) and Frankie (left) in the late 1950s.

Me (left) and Frankie (right) with a family member at
my grandmother's home.

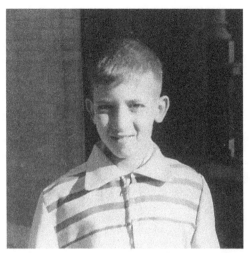

Me outside The House of Providence in May, 1956.

A photo of me (right) and Frankie (left) that
Carmella Grande kept with her in her wallet until
she passed away.

My grandmother's house in Syracuse.

A photo of my brother Frankie, some time in his
late teen years or early 20s.

A shot of the Fontainebleau during the time period that the crew and I would drive down and visit from New York.

Joseph and Carmella Grande celebrating their 50th anniversary.

When I first moved to Houston in 1982.

The House of Providence as it stands today.

One might wonder, "Where does an eight, nine or ten year old kid go when he's on his own?" I had been around Syracuse with the Grandes and with my grandmother, so I sort of knew where places were. I'd wander around the streets of downtown Syracuse. Sometimes I'd go off to some farms, play with the animals, swipe some food. Sometimes I'd find a playground, meet other kids and run around with my "new friends" until they had to go home. That was the best thing about running away; I didn't have anybody telling me I had to go home. It was my one true break from being ordered to do one menial activity to the next.

Sometimes the parents of the other kids would give me funny looks, wondering whose kid I was, but I didn't give a crap, I was free. I'd also go to Chappell's, Ridley's, W.T. Grant's and other department stores in Syracuse in the 1950s. Woolworth's was a huge store that took up an entire city block. It was a great place to warm up when it was getting cold outside and if the sales lady asked me who I was with or where my mother was, I'd just say she was upstairs shopping. Most department stores had toy departments where I'd find some stuff to play with for a while and, since the new televisions were always turned on, I'd watch TV. Sometimes I'd take one of the other kids from the orphanage with me but most of the time I'd go by myself. Of course, being a kid, I'd always go to the same places, which made it easy for the police to find me and take me back to House of Providence. It wasn't that hard to find a 65 pound kid wandering the streets by himself. The truth is, after several hours out on my own, I wanted to get caught and go back to where I'd get a hot meal and a warm place to sleep. Even I wasn't foolish enough to run away in the winter months. I liked being free, but not in the freezing cold.

Regardless of where I went, it wasn't without good reason that I left. Sure, I loved being free—that's something that has driven me to where I am now. After the Iron Curtain fell in Prussia, and the Hungarian nuns came to the House of Providence, I was running away more than ever.

The nuns from Hungary were a completely different story. These women—they thought we were spoiled brats! We were in an orphanage and they believed we lived in some sort of paradise. They had seen and experienced things we couldn't imagine, and they harbored the inner anger and fear that comes with an experience such as theirs even when living at The House of Providence. We were just little kids with no knowledge of the world outside of Syracuse; we didn't know why they were so spiteful towards us. They saw us as privileged. They saw The House of Providence as a mansion and us as ungrateful for getting to live in a four-story building, getting to go to school, having three square meals a day, and living in a place kept so clean that even lice breakouts didn't occur. To this day, I don't think they were really, truly nuns. They had to have joined the convent to come to America and escape the oppression in which they were living at the time.

Anyone from the older days who has ever been to Catholic school, or anyone raised in a Catholic orphanage will tell you that nuns and brothers weren't exactly kind to students or orphans. It's really the antithesis of how you'd think a man or woman of God would act toward children. A brother could yank a boy up by twisting his ear if he wasn't paying attention in class and no one would question why he treated the student that way. A sister could swat you with whatever she found handy at the time and leave a mark and no one would blink an eye. Take that type of disposition towards children and multiply it by any large number you wish, and it just about equals the mentality and actions of the nuns from Hungary. They didn't speak English, either, so the miscommunication occurring between them and us only made the entire situation worse.

As much as I hated being in an orphanage, years later I would realize that the food was actually pretty good and that I was lucky that I was in an orphanage in the United States of America, rather than in Africa, South America or Eastern Europe, where I probably would never have survived. There was no way to know then that The House of Providence was actually the best place for me, and every time I ran away, I was running away from the safest place I could be. Running away so often just upset the Hungarian nuns even more with regard to their attitude towards me. They took no mercy on me at all. They couldn't possibly understand why I would want to run away when I had it so good.

I had no idea I had it so good. In the regimented schedule of our time at the orphanage, we had a gym class where we all had to take part in whatever our gym teacher decided we needed to do that day. The gym teacher wasn't a brother or a nun; he was some guy they brought in specifically to teach us in gym. The gym was up on the second floor of the place where we went to school. One particular day, I angered the gym teacher. I don't know if it was something I said or something I did, but it upset him enough that he chucked a key chain full of large, old-school skeleton keys at me so hard that upon impact, I stumbled back and almost fell into the stairwell. He pitched it straight into my chest—so hard I had the air knocked out of me. I was stunned and so was everyone else. But I had a reputation to protect. So, I did what anyone would do; I picked the keys up and I hosed them right back at him, hitting him right above his eye on his brow bone.

The bleeding, miserably enraged gym teacher took me by my hair and dragged me across the gym to make a spectacle out of me. Every child was silent. They watched in horror as I held on to him with my little hands, trying to keep my hair—and dignity—in-tact. This man though, he was evil. He didn't just want to discipline me. He wanted to kill me. He took me out of the other door in the gym, lifted me up by my collar and threw me over the banister, a two-story fall. I landed right on my ass.

Mr. Destefeno, a school counselor for our social and emotional needs, came running out of his office, frantically asking what that sickening crack of a sound he heard was.

"It was me!" I said, plain as day. His face lost color and he stammered as he told me I could've died, and looking back, I'm surprised I didn't. He marched upstairs to the gym teacher and I heard them arguing loudly as I picked myself up off of the floor. My need to constantly run away was reaffirmed time and time again by situations like that one.

I constantly felt imprisoned and resented. I was never meant to be a caged animal—no one is—but regardless of my age or what resources I had available to me, I took action for myself.

I buried experiences like that deep with my memory. Some of the situations I was in I may never fully remember because I hid them so deep within my consciousness that I wouldn't have to remember if I didn't want to. No one wants to wake up each day and dwell on all of the shitty reasons they have to leave a place, or why they feel unloved. We may have had it better than orphans in other places, but we were still treated like less than second class citizens. Everyone, including my brother, handled it differently. What would anyone else expect? We were two totally different people. He seemed to internalize everything, and I ran from it—defied it. I openly spat in the face of the system in which I was trapped, but my brother took it all in and sought to comprehend the purpose of it all on some level.

For all of the down sides of living there, and the fact that the orphanage could never replace having a loving family, most of the American nuns at least tried to make life bearable. Besides being somewhat loving towards us, they even took us places once in a while. I remember a few times when they took us in buses down to New York City to see Broadway shows. When I was ten, in 1958, we saw the original West Side Story, about the two rival street gangs, one Italian and the other Puerto Rican. The many Puerto Rican Kids, and the few of us Italians kids in the crowd really liked the show, we related to it. I didn't know it then, but West Side Story would become one of the most famous Broadway musicals in history, and Chita Rivera, who we saw on stage, would go on to become a major star. We went other places too, like the Erie Canal Museum and the capital building in Albany.

Meanwhile, when we were back at the orphanage, my constant running away was turning into a very serious issue for the nuns. Everything was so regimented and carefully controlled, but I continued to escape. Sure, kids need structure in their lives—but this type of structure was extreme, especially for me. This was not the childhood most kids want or deserve. When it came to kids, we were the rejects, tossed aside or thrown away. Running away gave me a chance to have a taste of freedom and even have some fun for a little while. But, after two or three years of having the police bring me back to the orphanage, the nuns decided to teach me a lesson.

One night, after I had been out for five or six hours, I arrived back at the orphanage with my usual police escort only to find that my few items had been packed up in a small box which was waiting for me at the entrance. The nuns had run out of ideas to get me to stop running away. Lectures, discipline and corporal punishment had not worked. This time they meant business. I knew it, they were taking me to jail for real. Of course, since no one can legally take a twelve-year-old to a jail for adults, they took me to what was called a reformatory. This place made the orphanage look like summer camp for rich kids.

It was called Hillbrook Reformatory, and it was also in Syracuse. This was back around 1958. I don't think that building is still around anymore. I hope the inmates burned it to the ground—that's how much irreverence I developed for it. There is, however, a Hillbrook Juvenile Detention Center which opened in 1974. Different name, but probably the same horrible kind of place.

The first thing I remember were the bars on the windows and the locks on the doors. Instead of nuns keeping the kids in line, there were uniformed guards carrying nightsticks. When I arrived, everyone was in the yard doing exercises. There were maybe fifty kids, most were older, some looked mean, and others looked terrifying. These were not orphans, they were inmates. A kid had to do something seriously wrong to be there. Even then, I knew that running away from an orphanage was nothing compared to the stuff these guys must have done.

I looked around the place and looked at the kids outside. I wanted to say to the cops running the place, "Okay, I get it. I won't run away anymore. Now can I leave?" But I knew it wasn't going to be that easy. I was fairly certain I couldn't get out of this situation.

I was led to where we were kept, which were fairly small rooms, like cells, but with actual walls and four cots. They put me in with three kids my age, two were black and one was Italian, like me. One of the black kids showed me that he had a razor hidden in his shoe. He made it clear that he was in charge and that I was to stay out of his way at all times. I agreed, and didn't dare ask why he was there. The other black kid was a big heavy guy who liked to sleep a lot. He was probably the same age as me, but he must have weighed twice as much.

The Italian kid, Marco, told me he was there because he stole a car, then ran into a teacher he hated. He said he didn't kill him, but that he messed him up pretty badly. I wasn't sure if he was lying or not, but I didn't ask. One thing you learn growing up in an orphanage is that kids bullshit a lot, but you never call them out on it. This same rule holds true in places like reformatories. I told him I broke out of the orphanage about fifty times, which was true, and that once I stole a lot of valuable stuff from Woolworths, which was bullshit, but he thought it was cool. I don't think Woolworth's even sold anything valuable. I wouldn't say Marco and I became friends, but we got along well enough for survival in that place.

Everything was regimented to the extreme except for the fights. Instead of playing, like in the orphanage, we had to do an egregious amount of exercise.

There was no local school to go to; they had schooling in a study hall. The guards didn't give a shit if anyone passed or not, they were just there to kick an inmate's ass if he broke any rule or started any kind of trouble. These were really badass kids; they had been convicted of anything from stealing a car to aggravated assault or even murder. This was kid prison in the truest sense of the phrase.

I kept to myself, I was scared to death—I had thought I was a badass kid, but I was nothing next to these guys. I never murdered or maimed, or stole enough to count for anything. Anything I had ever done had been for my own survival. I wasn't a criminal. I knew my limits and I knew my boundaries, but I also knew I could outsmart most of them. This attribute helped me survive in that suppressive environment. There were a couple of kids in there that didn't like me, but I stayed away from them as much as possible. Between avoiding them, keeping my mouth shut, and essentially just doing what I had to do, I was able to escape the place without breaking through a door and running away.

Fortunately, I was only in there for two weeks. It was the longest two weeks of my life. Somehow, I survived. There's a Sean Penn movie called Bad Boys (the one from 1983, not the Will Smith movie). It's a pretty good film about life in a reformatory…or reform school as some people call it. I remember seeing it on television. Even though those kids were a bit older, it reminded me of those two horrific weeks of my life.

I never thought I'd be happy to be back at the House of Providence, but I was elated. These kids were no match for the kids in Hillbrook. Even going back to school was great. The only thing that worried me was my brother. Without me there to protect him, he had been beaten very badly one night and put into the infirmary. When I saw him, the bruises had gone down, and he was feeling much better and glad to see me. The nuns told me that even though he was doing fine, they wanted him to stay in the infirmary a little longer in order to get his strength up. I told him not to worry, I'd look out for him. There I was, his little brother, and even though we were polar opposites, I still tried to look out for him.

Life returned to normal—at least the only normal I ever knew. I was back in the orphanage, going to school, and still not being visited by anyone, ever. Deep down inside, I still felt like a piece of shit. But, at least I was better off than those kids in the reformatory.

Even the nauseating smell of sterilized cleaning was some sort of comfort upon returning.

After about three or four weeks back at the House of Providence, I remember heading to school one day. It was one of those bright, sunny, beautiful warm days, the kind that makes it almost irresistible not to enjoy rather than doing whatever the day's schedule calls for. I remember walking into the front door of the school and when nobody was looking, right out the back door. I ran away again.

Adding Insult to Injury: Paying Folks to be our "Parents"

Chapter 4

The nuns were completely stunned that I would dare run away again after my two weeks at the reformatory. I even surprised myself. I didn't want to end up back at Hellbrook, as I called it, but after a year at my grandmother's, six years in an orphanage, and two weeks in a hellhole, I really craved my freedom. The temptation of that beautiful day made it impossible not to enjoy. I had come to realize that for me, the best part of life was being out on my own, so I had to keep running away to get that fix of freedom.

This time, however, the nuns had a better idea. They decided to put my brother and me with a foster family. I couldn't figure out why a family would agree to take two teenage boys, especially one like me who was always getting in trouble. Then, one of the kids in the orphanage, who had been with about four foster families, explained that they gave these people money for taking us in.

It sounded like babysitting to me, but I figured what the hell, it's better than living in an orphanage forever. So, I would have people being paid to be my parents, I figured, why not give it a try? It wasn't that I had much of a choice, plus I had no other parents.

So, we were driven to the home of the Bellandi family. The nuns figured that since we were Italian we should be with an Italian family. I'm not sure why it really mattered, it wasn't like we spoke Italian or did anything culturally significant with regard to our Italian heritage.

The Bellandi's home was in Jamesville, about eight miles outside of Syracuse. It was a pretty nice place, a real small town of about 300 people at the time (1961). Today, there are about 30,000 people living in Jamesville. So, there we were, with Beatrice and Jacob Bellandi, their son Anthony, who was around my age and their sixteen year old daughter Lucia, who attended high school.

At this point I was already an adult in so many ways. Living in an orphanage makes a kid grow up fast. You don't have parents to do things for you or get you out of trouble. You have to take care of yourself. You have to watch your back and always be ready for the next smart ass kid who thinks he's king of the hill. Living with the Bellandis was going to be so much different. There were only two other kids in the house, not a hundred. I could handle this with my eyes closed.

Much to my surprise, they gave us a real bedroom on the second floor of the house with real twin beds, not cots. We were not living near a cellar with animals or any windowless dwelling of any kind. I thought maybe I could be friends with Anthony since he was about my age, but he was what would now be called a geek. This was the kind of kid who would do homework even if he didn't have any...you know the kind I mean.

Lucia was clearly not happy about us living there and totally ignored us most of the time. She was always putting on makeup and running off with her boyfriend. Thus, a sibling bond was not easily formed with these kids. Then there was my brother, who was still not very happy about his lot in life. He was starting to spend the majority of his time reading about God and religious things, on top of his normal routine of book study, which meant I would have to make my own fun.

Surprisingly, my fun ended up coming from attending school. I really liked going to Jamesville Elementary. At twelve, it was my final year in elementary school. The best part about it was that nobody knew me, so I could lie my ass off. I bullshitted about everything. As I had mentioned, bullshitting becomes a fine art of the orphanage life, and I was a pro after all of those years. I still had the orphanage mentality and I had learned that if I didn't bullshit, I'd get my ass kicked. So, this special skillset I had learned through painstaking instances over the years came in quite handy. No one in Jamesville could hold a candle to my abilities.

At Jamesville Elementary, I was popular! The kids really liked me. I didn't feel the hostility I always felt when I walked around in the orphanage. Where I had come from, there was always some tough kid who was pissed off because you were on his turf or some ridiculous load of crap. But not here; in this school everything was different. I remember the moment when my teacher first introduced me as Jimmy Fiume and told the kids that I was the new student in class. They all welcomed me and had smiled on their faces. These smiles were significant to me. They were genuine. It was so different than the orphanage, and it felt great.

I really liked gym class and playing ball outside with these kids. It was where I excelled the most, and incidentally where elementary popularity is usually established. I was more athletic than the other kids were because I had been competing with tough kids who were far more superior athletes.

For instance, playing basketball in the orphanage meant dealing with elbows to the face or hard fouls where someone would knock you to the floor, or even gym teachers that would throw you over a balcony to your death if you pissed them off. The kids in the orphanage made up their own rules and they played very hard, and there was no one around that cared enough to tell anyone any different. It was one of the only ways we could blow off some steam—and boy did we. So, by default, those of us who played developed into some pretty tough, competitive athletic boys.

Once I started attending school in foster care, I was competing with kids who were raised by parents who sheltered them. I overwhelmed these kids in sports. I intimated them, even though I was smaller than most of them. They looked up to me because I didn't back away from anybody. But the thing that made the biggest difference was that I wasn't a trouble maker or a bully. I was just being me. I knew that no one could bully me at this school—for once I was the king of the hill. I never had to actually say it; I just commanded it by the way I walked and the way I talked. I finally felt good about myself and finally had self-confidence.

It's sort of ironic that all those years of living life in a hellish orphanage ended up giving me the confidence I needed.

There was one guy, Steve, who had been the king of the hill until I got there.

But after we started playing sports and hanging out, he had nothing to say about me taking his "king of the hill" position from him. Even when Steve's girlfriend, Christine, showed that she liked me more than him, he really didn't care. He still wanted to hang around with me. That was the beauty of the whole situation—they couldn't figure me out. They all wondered, "Who is this guy? Why is he so balanced?"

I don't remember exactly how much I told them about my life, probably not very much. It was a small town, so perhaps some of them actually knew where I came from, or their parents figured it out and spread the word. But it didn't matter; the kids made up their own stories and those were the only stories that mattered.

Some thought I came from an orphanage, others thought I was straight from reform school and some even thought I had busted out of jail. Twelve-year-old kids have great imaginations and are terrific gossips. I didn't have to work very hard, my reputation came from them. I didn't have to say a word. It's like the old game of telephone. One kid says something to another kid, then that kid tells another, and the story gets mixed up and by the time everyone's been told something, everyone knows something slightly different. All it did was benefit me because no one would question me, and I had my bullshitting skills locked and loaded at all times.

I had a great time that year being a big fish in a small pond, or in a small town in this case. At home, things were very quiet. In comparison to my grandmother's home with animals underneath us in the cellar, my dad dropping by unexpectedly and customers stopping by at all hours for wine, this place was a morgue. I'm not sure if I subconsciously preferred the chaos to the quiet, but it just seemed unnatural. The Bellandis didn't talk much and when they did it was boring adult mumbling about whatever it was Mr. Bellandi did for a living or things going on in town or at church.

They didn't try and make us feel like family. They didn't let us call them mom and dad, like the Grandes did. Instead, we called them Mr. B and Mrs. B, since Bellandi seemed so formal to say all of the time. They took care of us, but they did the bare minimum. Mrs. B did our laundry and fed us, while Mr. B provided a roof over our heads. From a contractual standpoint, that was probably all that they were supposed to do. They probably thought they were doing us some huge Godly favor. But it wasn't like that. They weren't getting money to love us, just to take care of us. Since I was still pretty small for my age, I wondered if they got a discount for taking care of me, but I didn't ask.

One night, a night I'll never forget, I heard my brother sniffing and wiping his nose, trying his best to be quiet about it. When I went over to him, I could see he had been crying and I asked him what was wrong. He unobtrusively told me he was still very hungry, but we were already fed, cleaned up and in bed. It was true that they didn't give us a lot to eat, and we were two growing boys. Many Italian women love to cook and serve a ton of delicious food. Mrs. B was not one of those women. They didn't want to spend the money they earned for housing us on groceries. So, I figured I'd sneak out and get us some food. It wasn't easy getting out of there once I had gone upstairs to our bedroom. They all had rooms on that same floor too, and I knew at the very least the Bellandi kids were in their rooms. Often, Mr. and Mrs. B. were in the living room, which was at the foot of the stairs. That meant I'd have to find another way to get out of there.

As luck would have it, on that day it had snowed like crazy and there were large snow piles surrounding the house. Since we were on the second floor, I just opened the window and jumped out right into the snow pile to go and get some food. The store wasn't far, but I was worried that it might not be open after a snowstorm.

I was relieved when I saw the lights were still on. There were even a few other people in this little grocery store. I made my way around the store and stole some food for my brother and candy for myself. I'm pretty sure the store manager knew I was stealing but he didn't stop me; maybe he knew my situation. He just talked with the other customers as I slipped back out into the cold night.

I made my way down the street and got back to the Bellandi's house within the time frame of less than half an hour. I stopped in the driveway and looked up at our bedroom window, then I looked at the front door, then back up at the window. Not having planned ahead, I was stuck wondering how the hell I was going to get back in the house. What was I going to do, knock on the front door and say, "Hi, how is everyone doing tonight? Did you miss me? By the way, you don't feed us enough and my brother is upstairs crying from hunger pangs, so I went out and took care of it myself."

After some minutes of contemplation, I decided I could climb up the ladder Mr. B kept in the garage and get up to our window with the food. So, I went into the garage and dragged out their ladder. Since I was barely five feet tall and around 90 pounds at the age of thirteen, the old wooden ladder that was around ten feet long and heavy was quite the undertaking for me to sneak out of the garage.

Fortunately, the snow blanketed on the ground quieted the sound of me dragging the ladder around the side of the house where the window was. Now I had to somehow lift this thing up and lean it against the window without it slamming into the side of the house. Watching a five-foot-tall kid trying to steady a ten-foot-long ladder and get it up to the window, all while sliding around in the snow would probably go viral on YouTube. But in those days, there was no YouTube, or computers—we were lucky if we got to watch TV back in 1961. Finally, I somehow managed to get it up to the window. With the food stuffed in my pockets, I climbed back up to the second floor and through our bedroom window without making a ruckus. I put the food down on the floor between our beds and Frankie climbed out of bed to start eating. He didn't say thank you, but I could feel gratitude. I could feel his push and pull of emotion—not wanting to be looked after but needing it. Who would want to admit that they depended on their kid brother to sneak out of the house after a snow storm and steal food because they were hungry?

I reached out the window and pushed the ladder gently so it would fall back down. I figured that if I got up early enough, I could just go outside and drag it back to the garage. But as luck would have it, the family got up ahead of me. What I didn't realize was that when I pushed the ladder away from the window and back into the snow, part of it was sticking out into the driveway. So, when Mr. B backed his car out that morning, he felt the bump underneath him, and heard a loud clanking sound. Sure enough, he had driven over the ladder. I heard it and dashed over to look out the window. I quickly moved myself away from the window so he wouldn't see me, and I couldn't stop laughing. They knew it must have been me. I was still always getting into trouble, mostly little things, but that was the funniest thing I remember from my time at the Bellandi's house. If they were pissed at me, they deserved it. Don't starve my brother and I won't have to sneak out and end up ruining your ladder, I thought to myself.

We were there with the Bellandis for almost a year. When summer came, I was actually disappointed that school was over for the summer break. I had made some good friends in the neighborhood, but I really liked school because I was so popular—it was something I had never experienced before, and it was addictive and soothing to me all at the same time. I wanted to be back in school, it was much more fun than being at the Bellandi's house. There was no love in that home, at least not toward us. I'm not even sure if they loved each other—the environment was like living in a wax museum, nobody showed any emotion, and everyone seemed to move in a quieted stillness as though they just went through the motions without any real cognizance of what they were doing. As I later learned, my sentiments towards school ending were actually a common thing for kids who are in foster care. There is a tendency for children with bad home life situations to hate going home so much that they actually want to be in school, regardless of the behaviors they exhibit or whether or not they make good grades. School is where they have friends and generally a guarantee of safety and food—depending on the situation. There are exceptions to every rule, but I can attest to aligning with that mentality, and I understand what it feels like to be in the shoes of the kids who either currently are, or have been in foster care.

This reoccurring theme of no love was taking its toll. My grandma, the orphanage, and now the Bellandis were just about all I had to think of as family besides the Grandes, and out of the four, three were completely lacking real love toward Frankie and me. After the incident with Frankie being so hungry that it brought him to tears, I began acutely paying attention to everything that was being served to us, including the Bellandi kids. I remember that some of the food just didn't taste right, especially the potatoes and the milk. I soon figured out that we were eating stuff like powdered milk and packaged flake potatoes. At first, I gave Mr. and Mrs. B the benefit of the doubt as I thought maybe that's all they could afford. But after I had begun paying attention and made some connections in my head, it didn't add up since we got real, whole milk and real potatoes in the orphanage. In fact, the orphanage food was much better than what we were getting, and we even got more to eat at the orphanage. I didn't understand why food at an orphanage would be better and heartier than food at this family's home where they were earning money to take care of us.

Once I caught on to the milk and potatoes, I began noticing other things the Bellandis did that didn't add up. I noticed that her kids, Lucia and Anthony, were eating actual, real potatoes, and I even saw Anthony pouring himself a glass of regular milk right from the bottle. I was outraged! Mrs. B was getting money to take care of us and feed us properly, and yet there she was spending it to buy the best for her own family, of which we were clearly not a part. So, after calming myself down but still feeling riled at the fact that my brother and I were getting the shaft on food, I asked her, "Why do your kids have regular potatoes and regular milk while me and my brother are drinking powered milk and eating flake potatoes?" She told me it was none of my business, and that was the end of it.

I was completely exhausted of being treated badly. It had been seven years since we had left the Grande's home and I was still being treated like a second-class citizen. I really wanted to run away and find something better, because I knew intrinsically that there was something better. I woke up every single day knowing there was something better and I went out each day with the purpose of experiencing better.

I knew I had to leave this place. However, I didn't leave so fast this time. I had friends in the neighborhood and I spent a lot of time that summer playing baseball with them. It was just like you'd see in the movies. The neighborhood kids would all come out, mitts, balls and bats in hand, and we'd meet up and walk to the field together, laughing and playing with each other. That would be just about the only part of my childhood that was nostalgic.

I'd hang out with them and usually come home after my curfew which was around 8 o'clock. I figured if I had to live with foster parents that didn't really care about me, then why should I obey some stupid curfew?

During the summer, there were about five friends I hung out with frequently. One friend in particular was a Greek kid named Ted, whose dad owned a restaurant. Sometimes we'd stop in there after school and his dad would serve us the Greek food that he served in the restaurant. I wasn't sure what some of it was, but it was definitely much better food than anything I was getting at home. There was a lot of meat and potatoes in the food, and always some extra bread. I was getting better treatment after school from a friend's dad than I was in my own "loving home". It was nice of Ted's dad, but in turn it just reiterated what a crap deal my brother and I were getting from the Bellandis. In fact, I wanted my brother to be there with me, so he could eat something wholesome and have fun, too. But he kept himself quietly retreated, and didn't have friends like I did.

One summer night, a friend planned a sleep over party at his house. He had the kind of parents who would do something like that—the kind that don't mind a group of kids spending a whole night at their home and understood the fun we were having growing up together. Those kinds of parents are special. They understand what being a parent means and they just want to give love and good experiences to their kids. I had definitely never been to a sleepover and the whole idea enthralled me. It was like these parents were giving some sort of emancipation pass to kids! Even though we'd be under their watch, my friend's parents were so kind towards all of their son's friends that I had no doubt it would be an amazing time. I approached the Bellandis and asked permission to go to my friend's sleepover, but the Bellandis shot the entire notion of it down immediately. It was a hard and definite no.

My desire to go overwhelmed me and all my friends wanted me to be there, too. I felt I had earned a pass to a sleepover after growing up in an orphanage. This sort of opportunity for me at that time was like the equivalent to a trip to Disney World for a kid these days; it was something I had only heard about and knew that it was fun but never thought I'd be able to experience. I didn't understand why the Bellandis wouldn't just say yes. It was so easy, so simple. I'd be close to home, they'd know where I was, so I couldn't comprehend why the answer was such a cold-hearted "no".

I weighed the pros and cons. It would keep them from having to waste food on me, even the cheap food, and furthermore I would be out of their hair. Maybe they didn't trust me. Maybe they thought I would embarrass them somehow and tell all of the other kids how they really treated us. I didn't know what their reasons were, and frankly, I didn't care.

That night after dinner, I waited until the Bellandis were in the kitchen cleaning up. I looked around the house carefully and I went to the door, opened it quietly, and left. I headed straight to my friend's house, which was only about ten blocks away. I ran most of the way because I was anxious—anxious to get away from the Bellandis without getting caught and to finally get to experience a sleepover with real friends in someone's actual house.

The party was everything I had imagined it would be. I had so much fun. My friend's dad made some more of his delicious food and we devoured it. Some of the girls we knew from school came over. We put some popular records from that time (the early fifties) on the phonograph, played games and someone snuck in some beer—so for our age and at that time, it was like an adolescent frat party.

Even though I was thrilled we had something forbidden like beer available to us, I didn't really like it. I never was a big beer drinker, not back then. It was pretty late when the girls left. Once they were gone, we did what thirteen-year-old boys do; we made crude jokes, crude noises and told each other what we'd like to do with the girls. Then after some time and the small amount of beer we had was gone, we all fell asleep. The night had been a success.

The next day, I took off. I was impatient I guess, or I was just stupid; I ran away for two reasons. The first reason was the fake food the Bellandis gave us and the second was the fact that they wouldn't let me go to the sleepover. The reasons come across as superficial when they're spelled out so simply like that, but the two reasons had much deeper meaning. They were metaphorical of how the Bellandis perceived my existence. I wasn't worth feeding real food and I didn't deserve to have real friends. Since I knew how they felt about me, I knew that if I went back to their house after leaving without permission and tried to explain myself, I wouldn't be heard and the whole ordeal would be a nightmare for me, and I didn't want my brother to have to atone for any of my wrongdoing. The reason it was such a stupid move to run away from the Bellandi's, reg-

100

ardless of my second- class status in their household, was that I really liked school and the kids all liked me. I should have stuck around long enough to go to junior high school and play basketball and baseball with my friends. None of that swayed me, or even crossed my mind. I just wanted desperately to get away from the Bellandis.

Over the next few weeks, I went from house to house staying with friends. They lied for me as I made my way around Jamesville. It was still summer, so no one knew that I had decided I was not going back to school. I knew I couldn't go back to the Bellandi's house and I knew that I wouldn't be going back to school, but there was no way I was telling anyone any of the truth. After the summer had ended, I decided to just keep moving. I didn't want to return to the morgue where I felt I was living, and I had limited options. I ended up back in Syracuse. This time, at the age of almost fourteen, I was really out on the streets. Nobody could find me and I didn't want to be found. I was missing for about six months.

During that time, I learned to find shelter and keep myself warm and alive. I had to get creative and rotate around. I slept at the bus station, in an abandoned barn, and in a few sheds. I would also do some odd jobs in exchange for room and board and a place to clean myself up. One local food market offered me a cot in the back room if I swept the floors and unloaded the boxes. It was a fair deal to me, and I stayed there for a few cold weeks as it got closer to the winter. There was a heater in the back and that was great. I was lucky; I made some friends who hung out behind the market at night. They let me stay at their houses, telling their parents that I was a friend from school.

The streets teach lessons that can't be learned anywhere else. They whisper secrets into your soul that keep you from letting yourself die. I survived off of those secrets and I learned more than I ever would have from a book. I learned that when you are out on the streets, your first priority is food, then money and shelter. When I had to, I would swipe food, but I didn't swipe money. Instead, I always found some kind of work to do. Keeping a moral compass was important, too. I refused to let myself become a thug.

Eventually, after meandering from job to job, I made my way to the town of Lyncourt, where I got a job trimming the grass at a local cemetery. My grandmother was later buried in that same cemetery, but not for many years. I am not sure if it was coincidence or if it was some strange interweaving of the universe, but one day while I was out trimming grass, Joe and Carmella Grande came into the cemetery to visit Carmella's mom's grave. Although I hadn't seen them in years, I recognized them immediately as they walked across the manicured grass. They knew I had been placed in a foster home, and probably knew that I ran away.

Whether it was the Bellandi's house, the cops or even the orphanage, I think whoever was looking for me had possibly notified the Grandes that I had run away, thinking it possible that I may have gone back to their house. This, in turn, made them aware that I was missing, and possibly in a lot of danger. But there they were, and there I was. I couldn't believe my eyes. But before I could say anything to them, Carm saw me, gasped, and literally passed out on the ground. I ran over to her and Joe. We revived her, helped her up, and hugged. They were both so happy to see me, and to see that I was okay. It turned out that she had been notified that I was missing and that nobody could find me. A lot of people probably figured that I was dead. Yet, there I was, in a cemetery of all places.

We talked for a long while and I could see they felt terrible about the way things had turned out. They asked about my brother, who was still living with the Bellandis as far as I knew. Finally, after much resistance and me expressing my true feelings toward the situation, they talked me into going back to stay with my grandmother.

Besides the obvious reasons of not wanting to go back and live at my grandmother's, I didn't want to go because there the Grandes were right in front of me. They were my ideal parents. Why would I want to go back to my grandmother who had abandoned me before when I could see the Grandes and their clear concern for my well-being? These were the two people I could honestly call mom and dad. They didn't want me to go to my grandmother's, and they knew I would have preferred to have gone home with them. They were such wonderful people, but by that time they had already adopted one child, and with the responsibility of raising a small child, they had no room to take in an almost fourteen-year-old boy. So, they helped convince me that going to my grandmother's place was better than being a kid on the street, lost and thought to be dead.

They knew I loved them, but what they didn't realize was that they had been much more of a family to me than my grandparents ever were. The Grandes were still the only people who ever loved me. They would have adopted my brother and me, had my grandmother not screwed it up for us. No matter what happened throughout my life, from that moment on, I never let them disappear from me again. I always made sure I talked to them, visited with them, and helped them in any way I could. I stayed in touch with them until they passed away.

Before taking me back to my grandparent's house that day, the Grandes took me to a restaurant and we had a good hearty meal. We drove up to the big house where my grandmother was probably still making wine while my grandfather did absolutely nothing. The Grandes came in and visited with my grandmother, with no arguing this time. They stayed for a couple of hours and talked. I remember it being a pleasant visit, but I didn't want them to go. I reluctantly said my goodbyes to them when they had to leave.

From the outside of my grandmother's house, everything looked the same, but once I got inside I could see that things had changed. My grandmother was definitely much more forgetful, and she had slowed down significantly since I'd seen her several years ago. My grandfather couldn't slow down since he barely ever moved. I could sense that the last thing they needed was a teenager, especially one like me who really wanted my freedom. As it turned out, I was right. After a couple of months living with them, they shipped me off to live with, of all people, my father.

Pops

Chapter 5

My father wasn't exactly a changed man, but he had his own place and had somewhat of a routine established when Grandma sent me to him. I spent about nine months living at my father's house. It was a small house in an Italian neighborhood of Syracuse; nothing fancy, just a couple of bedrooms, a kitchen, living room, dining room, and a bathroom...most of it was not well kept, but I couldn't expect much more out of a father who was never there for me.

To my surprise, he was shacked up with his girlfriend, Evelyn, who was very attractive and several years younger than him. Dad had to have been about

35 and I'm guessing she was in her late 20s. She had a little baby girl, Daniella, who was not my father's kid. I wasn't entirely sure if she was with my father for a place to live or because she actually loved him. People that I knew saw her hanging out with other guys when my father was out of town gambling, which made me believe the former as opposed to the latter of my theories about their relationship.

All I had ever really known of my father was what I had seen living with my grandmother before the orphanage. I didn't know him. He was like a stranger to me; only a stranger that was somehow obliged to take care of me. I could take care of myself, and I didn't think too hard on it, but I did wonder why, exactly, my grandmother thought this was better for me than being with her. I was no angel, but I did my part to not drive her completely nuts. Now I was stuck with him—this stranger who I was supposed to know and call dad.

Life with my father was like living in a deranged frat house where I was constantly being hazed. It was a barrage of constant mistreatment, and dealing with him

110

being verbally and mentally. Meanwhile little Daniella had to witness it all.

He was constantly up to no good. The man was a real bullshitter, but not the same kind that I had learned to be from growing up the way I had. He was just an ice-cold son of a bitch. An ice cube could not have been colder than he was. His problem was that he was a small-time gambler and hustler who was not very good at it; kind of a "gangster wannabe". He could never truly run with the big guys. He had to pretend, talk big, and make it seem like he was of some importance. In doing so, he used and abused everyone around him. I could see why my grandmother really didn't want him staying with her, ever.

He hung around with shady characters like the guy who ran the cigar shop on our street corner, Angelo, who drove around in a Cadillac. You don't get a Cadillac from selling four or five cigars a day. Angelo always had some questionable business ideas to discuss with my father. I think the guy was a loan shark and the cigar store his front, and I'm not entirely too sure why he'd want to discuss business ideas with my father, as my father wasn't exactly the brightest light in the room. Nonetheless, Angelo was one of many characters and "associates" with whom my father "had business".

The only reason I stayed with him and Evelyn and didn't jet off into the void again was that I didn't want to get sent back to the orphanage or worse, the reformatory. Those memories were still too fresh, and I didn't want to live like that again. At least by living with him, I could come and go as I liked. Of course, that was only when I didn't have to babysit Daniella for Evelyn. It seemed that I always had to take care of Daniella when they went out, and they went out very often. Even though I really didn't like being a designated babysitter, I kind of felt bad for Daniella, with her having to grow up with them.

As for me, I was like a slave always being told what to do and never being acknowledged or appreciated or anything. This was actually worse than living in the orphanage, at least there we had good food and the nuns took us places. The nuns tried to make things a little better. My father clearly did not try at all. He didn't want me to be there, he only agreed to take me in because his mother could not deal with having anyone around, and because she still had some control over him. She was still more powerful in "the (gangster) community" and could make life more difficult for him if he did not listen.

I tried my best to live with them and stayed as long as I could. I even went to Grant Junior High School. They recently had a reunion and many of my old classmates remembered me, which means I was either very popular or a real pain in the ass. I liked school, mostly because I was happy to be away from my dad. The biggest conflict that was welling up within me was that despite my circumstances, I always naturally felt good about myself, and because my father was so negative and so cold, it was hard to actually be myself around him. I knew that my life sucked in so many ways, but I was not going to let living with my father threaten my positive outlook on life.

It just sucked to have someone in my ear constantly saying things to me like, "Hey, why in the hell are you smiling? You don't have shit to be happy about."

The only time I can ever recall a moment where my father wasn't a complete and total negative asshole to me was a time that I accidentally saw Evelyn changing, as she hadn't closed their bedroom door. Naturally, as I passed by and noticed I stopped to take a look. I couldn't help it, she was a beautiful woman (that I don't know how my father managed to keep around), and it was almost as if she had done it on purpose.

My father caught me looking. I thought, "This is it, he's about to kill me," and I prepared for the worst. Here I was, his son that he never gave any love to, and I was looking at his common-law wife as she changed clothes. But he didn't attack me. He didn't even curse at me. He actually smiled, as though he found the whole situation highly entertaining. I nervously smiled back at him and walked away. We didn't speak of it—but it was only that moment I can recall that he was almost behaving as a genuine, happy father toward me.

But what confusion I had! I didn't know if he was proud that I stopped to peek, or if he had such a lack of respect for Evelyn that he thought it wasn't worth being angry over. To this day, that moment baffles me.

There are reasons for everything, some known and some unknown. There had to be a reason deep within me that I still believed that a better life was out there someplace. It was a believe so deeply interwoven within me, so intrinsic and natural, that no matter what my circumstances were, I never doubted it for a moment. Even when I felt bad about myself and I had low self-esteem that I covered up, I still felt it. I believed it was the truth. Regardless of what crap my father pulled, I never wavered in my belief.

One evening, right after he was yelling at me about something completely asinine and ordering me to do another chore, I just snapped. I couldn't take it anymore. We were having dinner, and I just slammed my plate down and left the house. I honestly didn't care if I ever saw him or Evelyn again. I'm not sure, but Daniella may have ended up at an orphanage for girls. Poor Daniella, the orphanage may not have been a great place to be, but it was a step up from that awful environment.

Once again, at almost fifteen, I was back on the streets. Oddly enough, I wasn't on my own for very long.

Not long after returning to my nomadic lifestyle, I decided to go to a dance at the junior high school. I knew some of the other kids from school and it was nice to see them, but it was also nice to have some free food and a warm place to stay for a while. It was early fall and the weather was getting cold. I bumped into a girl there that I'd hung out with in school. I liked her, but I wasn't in any real position to take her on a date since I had no money and no home. So, we talked for a while and then she took off with a bunch of girls she was hanging around with.

I wandered around, ate a lot, and eventually decided to get going, but I had no place to go. I started slowly walking down the street from the school. It was windy, and the cold was hitting my face hard. Out of nowhere this guy drove up in a Cadillac and slowed down beside me. I recognized him from the neighborhood, his name was Tommy Gerardo. Everyone in the area knew Tommy. He was about 24 years old, the coolest guy around, with a fancy car, hot girlfriend, and a crew that followed him everywhere. So, Tommy rolled down the window and yelled out, "Hey, get in this car."

I remember yelling back over the sound of the car engine, "Is it warm?"

"Yeah, it's warm, now get in," he commanded back.

So I did. He asked me some questions and I told him I had no place to go, no mom or dad, and he told me he'd help me out. For some reason, he took me under his wing. Maybe it was his penitence. Maybe he had done so many bad things that this was his good deed, taking a kid off the streets and helping him out. He may have also seen me around and had known my story. Syracuse is a fairly large city, but like most cities, the people in any given neighborhood get to know who's who. Regardless of why, even if I was his personal atonement for his life decisions, I took him up on his offer to go with him.

So, I went back to Tommy's apartment, and he told me I could crash there for a few days. His girlfriend Lena was there, and she gave me some food. It was one of the few times I can ever remember that I wasn't hungry, having just come from the dance, but I wasn't going to turn down free food, so I swallowed it down.

That night was the beginning of one of the most memorable parts of my life, hanging with Tommy and his crew.

The Crew

Chapter 6

There was Butch, Joey, Richie, Adam, Tim and Eddie. Sometimes there were a few others that came and went. Like Tommy, they were all in their mid-twenties, about ten years older than me. From my perspective, these were much older guys, since I was still not quite fifteen.

I stayed with Tommy and Lena for a few weeks. I remember him showing me how to shave with an electric shaver. Imagine that, this twenty-something guy, real husky, a man's man and not my father, showing me how to shave. I only had peach fuzz sparsely growing on my face, so I couldn't get it right.

Since that didn't work, Tommy then showed me how to use a straight razor. He may not have been my father, and he sure as hell wasn't a father figure, but he really helped me.

Lena showed me a few things too. When Tommy would leave, she would usually be lying in bed. She'd kick off the sheets and there she was totally naked with the bedroom door wide open. Then she'd walk around the place in her robe, which she didn't always bother to close. She knew I was looking and wanted to show off. I was just happy to see what a full-grown naked woman looked like—without it being my father's girlfriend. We never said a word about it, it was just something marvelous that was able to experience.

Just a couple of days after he brought me in from the cold, Tommy told me to get in the car. This time, he took me to James Street where there was a Tastee Freeze on the corner. Tastee Freeze was a popular chain of ice cream and dessert shops that started in the early 1950s. There are still a number of Tastee Freeze franchises around the country. Tommy talked to the owner of the place, a friendly Greek guy, who said he needed a dishwasher. I was under-age, the guy wasn't even legally allowed to hire me, but he did. He was one of those guys who liked to act tough, but really wasn't. He explained the job to me and told me what hours I needed to be there. It was that simple. The cops weren't going to arrest him for hiring a kid, so I had my first real job. I liked working there, and pretty soon he taught me how to make sodas and sundaes as a soda jerk, making a few cents more an hour. It was 1962 and the average weekly salary was $128. I was probably making about $30 a week. As long as I could pay to rent a room, I was okay.

I remember Tommy coming in one night while I was there sweeping the floors. He asked me to make him a sundae, so I did, and I put in ice cream, syrup, nuts, hot fudge, and everything I could find in the place. He couldn't stop laughing, shrugging up and down with his big broad frame as he said, "That's not how you make a sundae." It looked like a sundae to me.

I kept that job for a while and it gave me enough money to afford a room in a rooming house. It was run by some older gentleman who had about eight rooms to rent out to people who needed them, and I definitely needed a place to stay. It was in a really nice neighborhood on Danforth Street in Syracuse. The room was small, but it had a bed and a dresser, plus there was heat. It was pretty much all I needed, and it cost about $20 a month. I stayed there for a few years, and my job gave me enough to afford it, so I was grateful.

Tommy was an interesting character. He was tough, but fair. He was primarily a hustler, a con artist, and a gambler, but unlike my father, he had a big personality and knew how to win people over. It helped that he always had a $100 bill in his pocket ready to pay someone to do something for him. He and the rest of the guys in the crew also had an incredible and almost uncanny knack for seeing what was coming at them. Since I had been a reformatory and an orphanage kid, I thought I was pretty knowledgeable about life and its grim realities, but when I hit the streets with these guys, it was totally different. I really thought I knew the streets from my brief time as a street kid, but I knew nothing compared to these guys. Some of them came from New York City, some from Canada, but they all knew the language of the streets, which is a language coded in ways that are ineffable to speak to outsiders and unintelligible to those who simply don't know it. As they were about ten years older, they had far more experience than I had. I learned a lot about life from the crew.

They all had cars, so they traveled a lot and let me come along. I went with them to the racetrack often; Aqueduct, Finger Lakes, and Saratoga. These guys knew how to bet and win. I wouldn't have been surprised if they had inside tips or knew that some of the races were fixed…or even fixed a few themselves.

We went to the Thousand Islands in northern New York State and to Niagara Falls, Rochester, and Buffalo. These guys knew people in every town we went to.

We ended up in a lot of pool halls, where they would walk in like they owned the joint. They'd play for a while, doing some small-time hustling, and then, after hours, they'd lock the doors and play for high stakes. They were amazing pool players. I watched and learned, and eventually I could run a few, but I was not like these guys, they could run three or four racks at a time. I remember this one guy, Cannonball, who hung out with the crew on occasion. He was a major hustler; he'd play 9-ball and give his opponent the 4, 5, 6, 7, and 8 balls, as long as he got to break. Then he'd break and he'd run the table. I can't emphasize enough how good they were—they blew my mind, as well as other people's wallets. They also knew how to bowl and would bet and win at the bowling alleys wherever we went. I was a teenager and was very impressed with these guys who were good at everything they did.

Tommy was a smooth talker, he knew people wherever we went and if he didn't know anyone, he'd still get us into places. Their ability to speak the language of the streets and their overall knack for winning people over with their lexicon of velvet smooth talking worked in every scenario in which they placed themselves. I wasn't privy to the private conversations they had, but whatever was said always seemed to work. They could get into any club, get a table at any nice restaurant, talk the money right out of a guy's pocket, and talk a girl into bed before she even realized they'd never call again—and I was the lucky young buck that got to tag along for all of it.

When they weren't playing pool, going to the track, or bowling, we'd go to the popular Jewish resorts in the Catskill Mountains where they had a lot of famous Jewish comedians like Shecky Greene, Red Buttons, Joey Bishop, Milton Berle, Buddy Hackett, Sid Caesar, Jackie Mason, and so many others. I didn't get to see all of those guys, but we saw many of them and laughed our butts off. Wherever we went we were treated very well. We'd go to Lake George in the summer and get the nicest cabins. We'd go down to Coney Island in Brooklyn, and even there they even knew people at the restaurants. I even remember going to shows at the famous Copacabana nightclub on 60th Street in Manhattan. I was still too young to get in, but I got in because I was with them.

Mind you, during this time I was not actually one of them, but they let me hang with them and go all over the place with them. I was sort of a gofer, or an intern, getting stuff for them or helping out with little things. For instance, we'd be at a bowling alley or in a pool hall and they'd give me some money to get burgers for them. They knew what the hamburgers cost, so they'd give me a little above the cost and I'd end up with perhaps twenty or thirty cents. Sometimes they'd buy me food, but not always, so I would often have to fend for myself.

A lot of the time, they would be going somewhere to make money through one means or another. A lot of "business" deals took place that they didn't tell me about. It was like a government "need to know" pass, and I didn't have one. I could see them heading into the back rooms, whispering, handing someone money, or doing some kind of business. They ran all sorts of illegal operations.

They would go to the local bus station and talk to young women who were by themselves carrying suitcases. I never heard their conversations with these girls but some of them would end up coming with us. I was never sure if the guys knew the girls would be there and the girls were sent to them from somewhere else, or if they just knew in their own way of knowing that these girls could be talked into whatever business the guys deemed appropriate.

There was one specific incident when I was living with Tommy that never quite left me. One night, they picked up this one cute girl at the bus station. They brought her back to one of their houses and there was almost an immediate understanding among them of what was about to take place. I didn't automatically see what was happening. I was about sixteen at the time, so I was merely going along with whatever they were doing, and they began taking turns having sex with her.

They encouraged me to go in and have sex with her too, but I couldn't bring myself to do it. From what I saw, which wasn't much, I couldn't tell if she wanted to be doing this or if they were raping her. They sent me into the room to be with her, but I didn't do anything, I simply couldn't do anything with her—I didn't have the heart. I knew intrinsically that it wasn't supposed to be that way. I stayed in there for a few minutes, long enough to make it seem like I had been with her, and then emerged from the room and told them an imaginative story of what had transpired. This is how I learned they were also pimping, among their many illegal activities.

A little later on, after I eventually told them that I didn't do anything with the girl from the bus station, they set me up to go downstairs at one of the pool halls and told me they had someone waiting for me. Evidently me confessing that I hadn't joined in with them on that particular night with the girl from the bus stop must have made them feel I needed to experience something of that nature. I went downstairs and discovered one of their hookers waiting for me. They had paid her to be with me. She seemed to be fine with the whole arrangement. She was very sweet and friendly, so I had my first sexual experience. It wasn't a bad one either—maybe a bit unorthodox, but it was what it was.

Even though that first encounter had been set up for me, I liked it and didn't mind so much about the circumstances. Pretty soon I started meeting some girls on my own. These were not ones that I'd have to pay, since I didn't have any money anyway. Some of these girls liked me because I was funny, but as soon as they found out I couldn't afford to take them any place, they would usually disappear.

Once, I did have an affair with a girl who did pay for everything. I guess she must have liked me. Nonetheless, never getting attached to anyone at that time was a huge blessing because it kept me from being chained to someone and getting into some serious situation that I had no business being in with a girl—not at that age and under my circumstances at the time.

In many ways, some of the guys in the streets were heartless criminals, but they were good to me. Maybe I reminded them of themselves ten years earlier. After all, they had been on the streets a long time. Looking back, the only thing that I can never seem to decide is whether they actually wanted me to be one of them and were grooming me or if they truly were just looking out for me.

There were some scams in which I played a minor role. For example, a friend of one of the guys, Leo from Florida, would be in town from time to time. He was an expert at forgery. So, in late April, or perhaps May, he would walk down streets in residential neighborhoods and take the brown envelopes out of people's mailboxes. These were tax refund envelopes with the blue checks inside, same as today. He would steal them and go to the social security office where he'd tell them he was so and so and get a new social security card in their name. He'd then forge the name on the check and have me go to the teller, whom he knew, and along with the social security card, cash the check.

He was probably screwing around with the teller or giving her a cut of the money, so she never asked any questions. I was just the messenger. The checks were often $400 or perhaps $500 and he'd give me some money for helping him out. I wasn't the forger, just the gofer, but it was a scam operation.

I became pretty popular around the neighborhood because I was hanging around with these guys. Even though, deep down inside I really didn't want to become one of them, being around them had its perks. Everyone knew them, and nobody was going to mess with me as long as I ran with them. Knowing them worked to my advantage.

I'd see high school kids coming home from school and I'd jump into the nearest telephone booth. Some kid would say hi and ask me what I was doing, so I'd say I was talking to Tommy. Of course, nobody was on the other end of the phone. Then I'd tell them that I was placing a bet for the track. Wanting to be cool and "in good with Tommy", kids would ask if they could place a bet, too. They'd always ask the same thing;

they'd ask if it was a sure thing, and I'd tell them, "Hey, I'm betting on it and so is Tommy." This set them up to immediately want to be a part of it. I'd ask, "How much you got?" The kid would say he had $8 or $9. So, I'd tell him that I didn't think he could bet an odd number ...they'd have to make it either $5 or $10. The kid would rummage through his pocket for more money and I'd ask, "You sure you want to do this?"

They were sure because they didn't want to punk out on Tommy and they'd hand over $5 or $10, so I'd place the bet with Tommy, or so they thought. These dummies didn't even ask what track or what horse. They were just so excited to be betting with Tommy. They were easy to fool because kids who were sheltered back then, and to some extent today, were so naïve when it came to street people. Their parents never taught them about hustlers, so they didn't know anything about life on the streets. Back in those days you didn't have to be as cautious as we are today. Nobody even locked their doors. This was before kids learned about so many things on television or on the internet, and long before the Walsh era of the 80s when everyone was checking their kid's Halloween candy for razor blades or fearful of kidnappers at every turn. There were some minor things, petty thefts that I took part in while I was with these guys. It's nothing I can ever be proud of doing, and I wasn't proud then, but it was a means to an end. If I could change it, I would, but I was just a kid trying to figure out how to survive.

Only once did I almost get involved in something that I really did not want to do. Remember, I was just a kid in total and complete survival mode. I was not looking to be part of a major crime or prove myself in that regard and I certainly did not ever plan on hurting anyone. However, I was around people that did hurt people and did all sorts of things that I couldn't and wouldn't do. I never harmed anybody physically, or even intended to. But there was one afternoon, when I was with Leo, the forger, and we had just left White Castle. As we were walking out, we spotted a guy, a little older than Leo, flashing a few $100 bills. I remember it vividly. Leo turned to me and said, "We've got to get his money."

My face changed and my brows furrowed a bit. I asked, "How are we going to get his money?" I was thinking that Leo had some clever plan to make up a story, talk to him, distract him, and take the money, or even come up with some plan to con him so he would just give us some of the money. But unlike the other members of the crew, Leo wasn't a good talker, nor was he as bright, so his plan was simple.

"We hit him over the head and take it," explained Leo.

That was his brilliant plan? Not wanting to sound weak or like a coward, I went along with his Neanderthal-like plan, but I really didn't want to have any part of it.

We headed toward this guy, but as we walked in his direction, he must have seen us so he took off running. Besides, some people can feel it—they know when something bad is headed their way. He scurried down the street and at the corner he made a left. Leo didn't see asked me which way he went.

I thought about it and told him that I saw him make a right. So, we turned right, and he was nowhere to be found. I really didn't want to catch up to him and was happy that we didn't. I still feel guilty about it today. I can't help but wonder what would have happened if we had caught up to him? I would have felt horrible. Every person has a line, some sort of moral compass that gives them a limit to what they can do to another human for no good reason—and that was mine. I'm so terribly grateful I wasn't put in the position to have to cross it.

Naturally, Tommy and the crew attracted attention from the cops. They knew lowlife operations were going on, but they were never able to pin anything on them. Now and then the police would pick me up, not for any of my minor discretions, like sneaking into movies with the crew to see Pink Panther films, or scamming naïve kids and taking their bets for the racetrack. Instead, they wanted me to tell them about

Tommy or some of the other guys. They were looking for me to rat them out, but I knew from the orphanage, the reformatory, and being out on the streets that you simply did not rat anyone out. I'd just say, "I don't know anything about them."

They'd ask, "What do you mean you don't know? You're always with them."

I'd say, "Yes, we go to the movies and to the bowling alley." The cops would give me a sandwich and a soda, and ask, "What do you do when you go to the bowling alley?" I'd be ready with an answer, "We BOWL!" I kept telling the cops that I didn't really know anything about them, which was somewhat true because they always kept me away from their true business dealings.

The truth is, while I liked hanging out with them and going places with them, I had to keep looking out for myself. I was just hustling for food—basic means of survival. I learned to play pool from them, but I was always a lousy bowler and an even worse gambler. They were always winning at the track. I'd ask, "How come you always win and I always lose?" They'd just hit me in the back of the head.

Hanging with the crew was fun, but when I wasn't with them, I was on the streets hustling for a few bucks here and there, doing odd jobs and just trying to survive. I needed enough money each month for rent, which wasn't too hard to get—remember my room only cost $20, and food was my top priority.

I wasn't really unhappy, but I had a heavy sense of loneliness, especially when the holidays came. Everyone would go be with their families, but I had no family to go and visit. Even most of the crew, and many of the people on the streets had people some place to go and someone to be with, but I was truly all alone. One time during a holiday I broke down and I went to visit my grandmother. She was pleasant, and the smell of her delicious homemade Italian sauce brought back a good feeling deep within me, but she didn't invite me to stay, which reminded me that there was no love. I was only there long enough to visit and then I knew it was time to leave. Even today, holidays make me sad.

Guardian Angels

Chapter 7

It was during the times when I wasn't with the crew that I had two experiences with what can only be described as guardian angels. No matter how deeply I have tried to rationalize it, there is no other way to explain what happened.

The first time I encountered this divine intervention, I remember being in Rochester, walking through some low-income housing projects. I'm not sure how I ended up in Rochester, which is almost 90 miles from Syracuse—I probably went there with the crew, but they must have been up to something that they didn't want me to be a part of, so as usual I was out on my own.

I was walking along, trying to stay warm and literally starving when I smelled food. It was a strong, enticing scent that took over my entire brain, making my mouth water. Its pull was magnetic, and I just kept walking toward this smell and ended up at a four-corner intersection. On one of the corners sat this really beat up tiny little dilapidated restaurant, with a few Black guys hanging around outside.

I just walked right up to this tiny restaurant and looked through the somewhat dirty window. Inside, I saw maybe a half dozen people at three tables with food on their plates. The guys out front stopped whatever they were doing to look at me and were probably thinking somebody threw away a perfectly good kid. God only knows what I must've looked like. I knew I looked pretty disheveled and I could see the pity in their eyes as they looked at me. I always hated being pitied, but in this case, I was too hungry to care. I was somewhere in between 14 and 15 years of age, in dirty clothes, with messy hair just peering in that window at the food on people's plates. Time had no meaning as I was standing there, it could've been five minutes, or twenty. I wouldn't have known because I was overwhelmed with my hunger, so I don't know how long I stared at everyone else eating before a heavy set Black woman in an apron, wearing her hair wrapped in a bandana came running out of that tiny place, grabbed me, and pulled me into the restaurant.

She threw me on the nearest wooden chair and said, "Boy, you sit there!" I wasn't about to move. I didn't know whether she was going to beat me for loitering or feed me.

Then, a few minutes into sitting there and staring at emptiness of the table in front of me, she came back carrying plates of collard greens, pig's feet, and all sorts of soul food. It was delicious. It was not food that I typically ate, so it was definitely different to me, but every bite was savory and completely satisfying.

When people describe a meal as soul food, I now know what they mean because of this experience. It didn't matter what kind of food it was. It wasn't about the exact type of food; it was about the whole experienc-

e. The food didn't just warm me up and fill my empty stomach; it touched me in a way that I felt deep within. It had a certain comfort about it that made me feel like I was at home, clean and wrapped in a warm blanket.

When I was all finished (and you better believe I finished every bite), she went out into the back alley behind the tiny restaurant and got into an old beat up car and signaled me to get in. So, I hopped into the car with her and off we went. She didn't say a word as she drove. I had lots of things I wanted to say to her in my mind, but I couldn't formulate any of those thoughts into words. I only knew I was overwhelmed with gratitude. She was a formidable presence, but nonetheless a Godsend.

She pulled off and parked on a street in a white neighborhood. It was like that back then, there wasn't much to think of her driving me into a white neighborhood because that was just how it was at the time. I remember that when I gotten out of the car I stepped onto the sidewalk, by the time I turned around she had driven off in silence, without ever uttering one word. It really happened, she never said goodbye to me or anything. She was a guardian angel who showed up when I was literally starving, gave me food, then disappeared.

There was another time back in Syracuse, when the crew was talking of doing something, most likely illegal, and I was on my own. I often went into Woolworth's on South Salina Street, because it was a huge store to walk around in, and a nice place to keep warm. On the main floor, there was a white refrigerated case with glass in front and food inside. On top was this glass rotisserie with hot dogs slowly turning while they cooked. It was like the inanimate rotisserie knew the pull it had by teasing a hungry person with its proud rotation. I can see it perfectly in my mind, the slowness of the rotisserie making the temptation of food more inexorable. Next to that was a machine with lemonade, grape juice, and orange juice. As I stood there and watched the hotdogs roast, I could feel the emptiness in my stomach consume me. I had no money with me, so I was trying to figure out how I could steal one of those hot dogs and run like hell.

There seemed to be no way to do it without causing an obvious stir and I was becoming desperate. Out of seemingly nowhere, there appeared an older lady, coming toward me from behind the counter where the hot dogs were cooking. I figured she was at least in her fifties, as she had that bluish-tone hair that, in those days, symbolized the archetypal sweet grandmother. Without saying one word to me, she reached into the rotisserie with those metal tongs they use to pull out hot dogs and she put it in a bun and on one of those paper hot dog holders. She sat it on top of the counter and then she took another hot dog and repeated the exact same act. Even more profoundly, she put a very light sliver of mustard on both of them and poured a cup of grape soda from the machine. It was beyond uncanny for me, because how would she possibly know that I usually put a sliver of mustard on my hot dogs and my favorite drink at the time was grape soda? During this entire episode, not a word was spoken between us and I had no idea for whom she was actually making the food. I looked to the left of me, to the right of me and behind me to see who ordered the hot dogs and the soda. There was nobody around in any direction. When I turned back to look at her, she was gone; she had disappeared. But damn it, the perfectly crafted hot dogs and the bubbling grape soda were right there in front of me, so I grabbed everything and I slowly walked away and kept walking right out of the store. Nobody touched me. Nobody spoke even to me, and just like the day I was given the soul food, nothing I could have purchased tasted quite as good as this gift from seemingly nowhere.

Those were the two strangest stories from my days on the streets. I had no other way to explain them, so I figured that apparently, I had two guardian angels, or at least one that could appear at different times in different places and look completely different.

Aging Out of the Crew

Chapter 8

Life on the street was difficult, but the crew made it more interesting. Once, we took a road trip down to Florida. I was about 17 at the time, and we drove down in a couple of days. We stayed at the Fontainebleau, the most luxurious hotel in Miami Beach. The 1,500-room hotel opened in 1954, had twelve restaurants, and major name performers on stage almost every night. Frank Sinatra and Dean Martin would play there, and we got to see Jackie Gleason who had made his mark on TV with The Honeymooners.

For me, this was another world. I'd never even seen a palm tree before. The weather was warm, the girls in their bikinis looked great, and it was on this first trip that I fell in love with Florida. The concierge and everyone who worked there treated all of us like gold. They referred to us as "the guys from upstate"; well, not me, since I was just tagging along; but Tommy and the gang were well known some 1,200 miles away from Syracuse. Even in Florida, they went to the dog track and won. It wasn't just luck, they knew something about betting on the dogs, but I never dared ask what they were up to. As long as I had a place to sleep and food to eat, I was content with having no insider knowledge.

By this time, this was a crew of guys who were now in their late twenties and ran a variety of illegal operations. They were not a gang with some kind of initiation ritual or a reputation for gang violence while looking to defend "their territory". But as it goes with any group that worked the way they did, there were people they would piss off along the way and occasionally fights would occur. In one case, not long after our Florida trip, another crew of a comparable lifestyle decided to try to take down Tommy and the boys. As always, the guys saw trouble coming and they were fully prepared.

We were in a luncheonette very late at night, probably around 1 or 2 A.M. Sometimes after a night out they would stop somewhere to get a bite to eat, often an "early" breakfast. There were about six of us sitting there, including me. They got me something to eat, and were just hanging out when Tommy suddenly stopped what he was doing and said, "Jim you've gotta leave." I told him I didn't want to leave, but he was adamant that I get out of there immediately.

"Jim, you gotta get out of here right now!" he commanded.

When Tommy was serious I knew he meant business, so I went across the street to the Brown Jug, a bar where we spent a lot of time drinking, and the crew would do some "business". The place was emptying out, but I was just going to hang out there for a little while, until whatever was going on with the crew was over. There was also a waitress there that I liked. She knew I was underage, but she also knew I hung with the crew, so it was okay for me to stay there for a while.

After spending nearly an hour talking to the waitress, I went back outside, but there was nobody around. The streets were eerily quiet, so I walked back to my place at the rooming house about a mile away. The crew never came looking for me, so the next day, I went out to find them. A few of the guys were at one of the local hangouts. I asked what happened the night before. They told me there had been a big fight and that Butch got in trouble. Then they handed me a newspaper and it was all right there in black and white. Apparently, these other guys were looking to make a name for themselves in the area, but Tommy and the crew beat the crap out of them. I put the paper down and they filled me in on some of the details that had been left out of the news.

Butch had taken a ketchup bottle, broken it in half, shoved it in a guy's face and twisted it around, tearing his face up. The guy almost died. Butch ended up getting arrested.

Tommy had taught me long ago that when you're in a street fight, you fight to win, whatever it takes. There are no rules and no referee like in a boxing match. If you show weakness, you'll lose the fight and you could get killed. These guys showed up ready to have a fistfight. Tommy and his crew used baseball bats, knives—whatever they had in order to fight to win. They didn't look for fights, but when challenged, they fought, and fought hard, very hard. They did whatever they had to in order to always win.

Most people in Syracuse knew what Tommy and the crew were capable of doing, so the guys were rarely challenged. They had long established a reputation before I started hanging out with them. I remember one time my brother was in the neighborhood, probably heading to visit our grandmother. I had only seen him a couple of times since I left the Bellandi's home, a few years earlier. I was walking along Salina Street with the crew. He came running up to me and told me that some guys were bothering him. It was a bunch of hoodlum kids in the street who were following him and making threats because of his sexuality. I felt sorry for him because it was a very rough time for him to be in that position. He was fragile, both emotionally and physically. Tough kids would always make fun of him. Even though I was embarrassed, I remember telling the crew that my brother was in trouble. So, we walked toward the hoodlums and the second they saw us, they took off without a word.

When I was about 17, Tommy and the guys decided they were tired of going to other people's clubs, bars, and dances, so they opened their own place and named it the Coronado Club. I didn't know where they got the money, and it's probably better that I didn't know. The club was quite impressive. It was a big place on the west side of Syracuse, a so-so neighborhood where some of the lower middle class lived. We were all from north side of Syracuse, the Italian area which was more of a working-class neighborhood. They gave me a job checking people's ID cards at the door before they could enter. You had to be over 18, which was the legal drinking age at the time. It was ironic that I was telling people that they had to be eighteen to get in and I was only seventeen.

The guys went all out to make this place impressive. Fancy décor, a big dance floor, a very long bar, and some back offices where who knows what kind of deals were going down. There were plenty of interesting characters heading back there. From the looks of it, there was a mix of mobster-types; "associates", bookmakers, bootleggers, talent bookers, hookers, and others who I had no idea what they were up to. The cops came by from time to time, but the guys made sure everything was on the up and up, or at least appeared that way.

Late one night as I was watching the door, the waitress I liked from the Brown Jug came into the club. Since I had first met her, we had developed a relationship. It wouldn't be what you would call "boyfriend and girlfriend", but we had some good times together—a lot of good times. It didn't seem to bother her that I was a few years younger than her, she never hesitated to be with me. She was about 21 at the time, and we hadn't seen each other in a few weeks before that night. I liked her, I was ready to see her again so I was pretty happy when she showed up. She saw me, and since not too many people were coming in at the time, we were able to talk for a little while without interruption. She had not been to the Coronado club before and wanted to check out the place. I had her on my arm and I escorted her around proudly, giving her the grand tour, then I had to get back to my post. After about an hour, I was finished working up front and I started looking around for her. I was looking forward to hooking up with her again that night. I had missed her, yet every place I looked, she was no place to be found. I figured she must have had to leave in a hurry, and didn't have time to say goodbye.

As I was thinking about it and had come to the conclusion that she must have left quickly, something caught my attention toward the back. That's when I saw her emerge from the back offices with one of the guys from the crew. The two of them were laughing and holding drinks as they left together. It was about three in the morning and she didn't see me.

I was pissed; he knew I liked her, knew we had been together, and knew that we were more than a one-time deal, but he didn't give a shit. There was no 'bros before hoes' where I was concerned. I knew at that moment, more so than ever, that I wasn't part of the crew and never would be. Apparently from their point of view, regardless of how loyal I was or what I did for them, I was just some teenager hanging around with them, following them, doing gofer errands for them. I had had a lot of fun traveling all over with them and learned invaluable lessons about life. I knew that Tommy had pulled me off the street when I really needed some help. I always appreciated that, and I will never forget it, but I wasn't fourteen years old anymore, I was nearly eighteen. I couldn't tag along with these guys to pool halls, the racetrack, and work for them at the Coronado Club forever. I had outgrown them and clearly, they had outgrown me. It was time to go my own way, even if it meant going back on the streets.

There was that feeling inside that I could do better than this. I was the kind of person that woke up every day and knew I wanted to do something I wanted to do, regardless of what anyone else wanted to do. I was determined, each and every day, to have a good time. I didn't want to be a hustler, a gambler, a pimp, or get into any of the things these guys were doing. Something better was going to happen in my life, but not if I was always hanging around with these guys. My days in the crew had come to an end.

Once again, I was back on the streets, hustling and trying harder to get some work. I was able to get jobs more easily now that I was older, so I worked as a painter's assistant, and as a painter, at a dry cleaner's, and did day jobs brushing down the tables at pool halls, cleaning up at a local luncheonette, and so forth. I was still pretty popular around the neighborhood. Even though I was no longer hanging out with the crew, people thought I still was and that carried some weight. Between the small hustles and the jobs, I was actually able to afford to move out of the rooming house and into my first apartment which I shared with Leo, who had moved up from Florida. Leo was still doing his own hustling, but I steered clear and worked at my day jobs. The two of us managed as roommates just fine.

I remember not long after we moved in, when I was still eighteen, Leo and I went to White Castle along with his brother who was visiting from Florida. While we were there, about six Black guys started making fun of Leo and his brother's Southern accent and throwing pennies at them; I'm not sure why other than it was the time in which we lived. Leo was a tough Italian who didn't take shit from anyone, so when one of the guys suggested taking it outside, Leo went. His brother stayed behind and so did I at first. But as the five other guys followed their friend outside, I got nervous. I knew it wasn't going to be a one on one fight—I had learned the streets don't fight fair. They were going to jump him.

I asked his brother, "Don't you think we should go outside and see what's going on?"

His brother shook his head "no", but I was not going to be a coward. I learned from the orphanage that being a coward hurt worse than any beating I was going to get. So, I went outside myself and sure enough they were all beating the shit out of Leo. I let out a yell to get some of the attention away from Leo and jumped on the pile. I was still a little guy and knew I was going to get hit hard, but I was not going to be a coward. Then all of a sudden, the fight stopped and I saw a bunch of Marines tossing these guys off of us like tin cans, and they beat the crap out of these guys. Leo and I thanked them and headed home with his cowardly brother.

It was also around that time that I had met some Marines who had returned from Vietnam. Over the years, I'd known a few guys who got drafted, including some who did not return. At this point, it was the mid-sixties and the war was escalating. I was not about to be drafted. When you're out on the streets no one can get a hold of you, it's a little hard to receive a draft letter. It wasn't like I had an address or even a Social Security number. One of the guys I met was on leave. I remember him telling me that I should come to Vietnam. He told me that he was a bartender in Da Nang, in the Marine Corps, adding, "You gotta come here, free food, girls, drinking, it's great over here." He was making it sound like a summer resort, but there was also this war going on. Even still, I wanted to go to be part of the action. So, I went to the Marine recruiting office—at that time I was still about 5'4" and 100 pounds. I walked into the recruiting office and the officer at the desk asked me, "Can I help you?"

I said, "Yeah, I want to join the Marine Corps." He took one hard look at me and said "Boy, you're too light to fight and too thin to win... try the Navy." I didn't bother trying the Navy, clearly I was not getting into the military.

Hitting the Road

Chapter 9

A few years later, in 1972, at the age of 24, I would pick up and leave New York. Before I left, I made one last attempt at a domesticated life that ended up wreaking havoc.

I was nineteen years old. Who was I to get married? I could barely take care of myself. I had just come off the streets, took a job at a factory, and decided to get married. It was all impulsive and stupid. I didn't make much of a husband since I had no idea how to be one, or start a family, or any of that stuff at 19 years of age. Remember, I didn't know anything about a loving relationship or a real family. I had absolutely no role models for that type of life.

All I had ever known was trying to take care of myself and survive on the streets. It was like trying to take a wild animal and make them a domestic pet. Not easy to do. You can't tame a wild thing if they're truly wild at heart—they will always be that way, and if you back them into a corner, they'll claw their way to escape.

I tried to be married. I worked. I came home, I went through the motions, I tried to be the person that society taught young men to be, but I had gotten myself into this situation for all of the wrong reasons. Now I was trapped. I kept torturing myself over and over because I realized I'd backed myself into this corner. I was the one who had seen this beautiful girl, Michela, and gone for it. I was the one who didn't think the whole thing through and decided to be married so impulsively. Sure, Michela went along with it and didn't question it—most immigrant women at that time wouldn't question it. To no fault of her own, she was living with a man whose whole self was about to explode because he realized how horrible of a husband he was.

There was this one time that Michela had cooked a big meal for the two of us and was waiting for me to get home to eat. I didn't think another second about hanging out with some of my friends instead of going home. It wasn't that I was deliberately trying to be disrespectful to Michela, I just wasn't thinking of her...I was only able to think about myself. When I got home, it was around three in the morning. I remember being so pissed because food was not cheap and she'd left everything out, set on the table to spoil, and had gone to bed. She hadn't even eaten hers. My anger quickly turned to sadness. I was completely conflicted. When she woke up the next day, she didn't speak a word to me. She just went into the kitchen and cleaned up everything, dumping out all of the spoiled food. It was her way of saying, "Screw you, if you don't come home, the money you make that goes towards food is going to waste."

The tension between Michela and me was growing. I don't know if Michela said something to her grandmother, but my grandmother tried to talk to me about it one day, but not much. She wasn't big on talking to any of us and clearly never made my father a good husband, but she said something along the lines of "I told you so," and I was pissed at that, too.

I didn't like people telling me what to do or what was good for me. I had to learn on my own that marrying Michela was a huge mistake.

I was good with women. I was a nice guy, I was never the bad guy. But somehow, I had screwed this up and I was Michela's bad guy. I could see it in her eyes. She was wounded by the way I would treat her. I'm not talking about violence—she was wounded by me ignoring her constantly and not treating her like a wife should be treated. I would blame her for the most innocuous things. I may not have been violent in the typical sense, but I'm sure I did a number on her psychologically. I knew I was the one who screwed up, but I refused to outwardly acknowledge that and instead, I would just blame, blame, blame. It was her fault—anyone else's fault—for anything that happened

164

…but I wouldn't let it be mine. If I stayed out late and didn't come home, it was because I said she made me feel trapped. If I talked to other women, I lied and said it was because she ignored me or didn't make me feel wanted. I wouldn't tell anyone that I was the one acting out because I was miserable and I knew I was in the wrong. Being the bad guy bothered me as much as not having my freedom. It was a recipe for disaster.

I could feel it intrinsically and it grew worse every day. I was dying inside. I was in the wrong place and I knew it. I was the type of person who woke up every day and wanted to do what made me happy, what I wanted to do. That had been the running theme of my life up until I married Michela. I know it seems incredibly selfish, and it was incredibly selfish, but it was just the way I was. I had been that way as long as I could remember—even at the orphanage, it didn't matter what I was supposed to do, I did what gave me joy. So, living in this contrived world of marriage and happy husband and father life was not truly for me. I couldn't wake up each day and do exactly what I wanted. I had to explain myself, or ask permission, or worse—just not do what I wanted to do.

So what does a caged wild animal do when it's released? I woke up one day, feeling the truth within my soul, knowing that the life I was living with a woman who didn't deserve some jerk like me wasn't fair to her. I decided right then and there that I had to leave—not just leave her, but leave three beautiful children.

Everywhere I looked, all I saw were painful memories of being hungry, homeless or orphaned. There was nothing for me there anymore—not that there ever had been—and I wasn't doing Michela or the kids any favors by keeping them in an unhappy relationship.

I was 24 when I left. I didn't lose anything in the divorce settlement because I had nothing. I actually felt badly for her because she got the worst end of the deal. She married someone straight off the streets, and that simply does not work out very well.

The first thing I did was go out and buy a new MGB. What else was I supposed to do with my newfound freedom? These were the hottest sports cars of the '70s, made in Great Britain. Today they sell for a lot of money at classic car shows. They weren't cheap back at that time either, and I had no money. I got a friend to help me by putting the car payments on a credit card. Since I couldn't make the payments, I knew they would eventually repossess the car, but they'd have to find me first.

I set my sights on traveling to Arizona where I knew my Aunt Rose was living at the time, hoping I could stay with her for a little while. Even though it was a bit out of the way, I wanted to follow Route 66, which was the name of a very popular TV show back in the early '60s about two buddies who traveled across-country in a Corvette. Each week they were in a different location. I couldn't think of a better way to head west. I'd have to make the journey alone, but that was perfectly fine by me; I had been alone before and I could do it again easily.

The anxiousness I had to get out of New York provoked me just as much as the excitement of the trip ahead. I had to get out of the place that kept dragging me under like a tidal wave and pulling me through a rip current back to square one over and over again. The first thing I did before I set out on the road was buy a map at a local gas station. I started out on the road with $10 in my pocket, which would only be around $60 today. It wasn't much, but I was so happy to be hitting the road that it didn't matter to me. I had survival skills. There's a saying about New York, "If you can make it there, you can make it anywhere." Well, I didn't make it in New York and I was happy to leave.

It was amazing how the pressure and the bad memories seemed to lift off of me when I got out on my own and away from New York. I couldn't help thinking I'd never see snow again or be cold again. I could start all over again in a warm climate. Nobody would know if I was an orphan, had a mom and dad, or if I was rich or poor. I didn't have to talk about my family, the orphanage, life on the streets, or anything if I didn't want to. I felt an overwhelming sense of freedom, even rejuvenation. This was a moment of real happiness for me. This defined who I truly was; it was my ultimate new start.

All of the years I spent on the street and all of my experiences with the crew were exactly the type of training I needed to head off on my own. In order to set out on my cross-country journey with nothing but a sports car and my wits about me, everything I had picked up in my years of hard earned resilience paid off. I learned from Tommy and the crew how to size up people, how to schmooze and start up a conversation with almost anyone. I was not as good as those guys at seeing everything coming at me, but I was a lot better than most people. The other thing going for me was that I was loaded with confidence. I knew I could always get a job and a tank full of gas when I ran out of money, which wouldn't be long with $10 in my pocket. Digging ditches, cleaning tables at a bar or a restaurant, washing dishes, whatever job I could start at right away, I would take.

I also had a plan. I was going to stop in small towns along the way, and network to meet people and get jobs. This is kind of like what people do today, except they find each other online and meet for lunch or at Starbucks. I was going to walk into bars, taverns, or inns to meet the locals in each town and start up conversations. This would lead to day jobs and perhaps some place to sleep, although the car would always suffice, and very often it served as my bedroom. I figured out early on my trip that if I slept in my car, I could then look for a hotel or a YMCA the next morning, where I could find the men's locker room and shower and clean myself up. Remember, security at that time was nothing like it is today with passes and entry codes to get into places.

After about six hours, my first day on the road, I was somewhere in Maryland. It felt so good to be out of New York and on my own. I felt like I could actually breathe. This was my ultimate freedom, the thing which I had always desired most—why I kept running away from the orphanage. I could do whatever I wanted.

170

I decided to turn off the main road and stop at the first town I saw. It was early evening and I drove about 20 minutes until I found a small town. Then I slowed down to look for a bar. Sure enough, there was a sign for a tavern on a corner. So, I parked and strolled inside. The place wasn't very crowded but there were maybe half a dozen guys sitting at the bar. I ordered a beer for about a dollar, in some cases, I later learned along my journey, you could get a special two for $1 beer offer. Actually, I was usually okay with one beer, I knew the art of nursing a beer for a while to save money, and as I mentioned earlier, I was never really a big beer drinker anyway. If I saw beer nuts, pretzels, or something like that on the bar I'd ask someone to pass them my way. They would pass them down and I'd say thanks and ask if the place was always that quiet, or busy, depending on where I was. In most cases that was all it would take, just some simple question to start up a conversation. People are usually pretty relaxed at a bar, and I knew that once you got them talking you could learn a little about them.

I also knew how much people love talking about themselves, heck I love talking about myself, too. So, they would talk for a bit and then ask me about myself. Since nobody knew me, I could tell them anything, and boy did I ever. Sometimes I'd even attract a crowd of folks who wanted to listen to my stories.

By the time I left that first bar in Maryland, I had made a friend of a guy at the bar who came in and joined us. When I mentioned that I was looking for some day-to-day work he gave me his brother's phone number to call, and the next day I was painting fences on his brother's farm on the outskirts of town. It was a job for three days, with three days of pay, which was enough to get me food and a tank of gas. In those days I could fill the tank of the MGB for only $3.50.

I found a bar in every town I visited. Some were just small, local watering holes, others were old Irish taverns, VFWs in the south, and there were a few places that had musicians playing and others that just played records for dancing. In fact, the further south I got, the more country music was being played by live groups.

Regardless of what type of music a place played or where I found myself, each place all had one thing in common—there were always people coming in to get a drink and usually socialize. Bars back then were nothing like the typical bar that one would see today. There were no big screen televisions all over the place, no virtual distractions of sports or anything else, so people needed to make their own entertainment, and if they were alone, like me, that meant striking up conversations.

I would estimate that close to 80 percent of the folks I met in bars were friendly, and in most cases, someone had some work for me, even if it just meant sweeping up the bar at three in the morning after everyone left. But not every place I walked into was inviting. If the place seemed unfriendly, or hostile, I simply turned around and left. Since I was going to be following Route 66 across the country through the south, I also learned that having a sports car with New York plates might not play well for me with the Yankee haters from the south. So, to play it safe, I'd park my car a block or two away from the bar or tavern. I remember walking into one place and staring at a huge confederate flag. The bartender had a confederate hat on and I thought to myself, "Maybe this is not a good place for a Yankee."

I vividly recall going into a few other places where I immediately noticed that the patrons were looking at me like they wanted to kick my ass and I knew it was time to get out. Remember, being on the streets had heightened my awareness of what was going on around me. On the streets, it's important to keep your eyes and ears open so you can see what's coming at you. I remember at one bar I saw six guys from a biker gang come strolling in, and I knew this was my cue to go strolling out. I was by myself, not looking for trouble and without a crew with me, so I had to be aware at all times when I wasn't welcome or when someone posed a threat. It was another lesson I could have only gleaned from the streets.

As I continued west, I must have stopped in 30 towns, and found jobs in almost all of them. One guy liked having me hanging around the bar so much that he offered me a job. I said sure, and worked as a bartender for nearly a week. Most people wanted beer, a few wanted wine, and if someone wanted a mixed drink I'd make it if I knew how from watching the bartender at the Coronado Club. If I didn't know how to make it, I'd look around the bar then tell him I didn't have all the ingredients. A simple, "We ran out," and most people would settle for a beer.

A lot of the bars had music on, sometimes for dancing. I had been in a lot of bars over the years and had learned to dance. In one southern bar, some girl reached out, grabbed my hand, and pulled me onto the dance floor. So, we were doing whatever the popular dance was at the time. Imagine a seventies-style jam playing and me and this pretty girl perfecting the moves out on the dance floor for everyone to see. While we were out there on the dance floor, I noticed a rather big guy watching me closely with a pretty nasty look. Then he leaned over and said something to his friend. So now there were two big guys watching me with pretty nasty looks. I'm said to myself, "One of these guys may be her boyfriend."

When the song ended, I put my arm around her to walk her off the dance floor and she leaned in and said, "I think you'd better leave." I glanced over to the two guys who were basically looking at me like they were going to kill me. At that moment, I remembered a saying from the streets, "Life doesn't suffer fools." When I first heard it, I asked Tommy what the heck that meant. He said, "It means don't be stupid."

I learned that you have to know when to get the hell out of danger, and this girl was telling me it was the time to get out of there, so I smiled at her, said a quick goodbye and left. It was too bad because I think she liked me.

You also learn on the streets that you can be a tough guy, but tough guys can get killed too, so you have to know when to get out of a bad situation. I never wanted to be a coward, but this was not about standing up for myself, my buddies, or my country, this was some bar in the middle of some town, somewhere along Route 66, and I was not going to get in the middle of whatever was going on.

Meanwhile, my resume was growing quickly as I made my way down the road. I worked as a dishwasher in a few of places, and at one place they asked if I could be a fry cook and make hamburgers. I figured, how hard could it be? You throw the damn thing on the grill, put a little bit of lard on there—people used lard in those days—then you turn it over a few times, put some lettuce and tomato on it, put it on a bun, and there you have it. People would say, "Man you know how to cook!" and I'd just smile thinking, "You've gotta be kidding me." People don't stop to think about how easy it is to cook a hamburger. It's not just about the hamburger, it's one of those things that people don't realize about life. If you want to make it happen, you make it happen. If I needed to make a hamburger, I made a hamburger. I didn't overcomplicate things. One of the worst mistakes a person can make is overcomplicating the simple things and getting stuck in one gear, then they never get past that.

I met another guy who asked me to basket eggs on his farm. At first, I wasn't sure what that meant. Then he explained to me that it meant putting the fresh eggs from the hens into a basket. Talk about your mindless job. This was as easy as a job could get, except for one little thing—roosters are not happy when you take the eggs away from the hens. I remember one time when I was chased by this giant rooster that was hell bent on killing me. I had no idea how vicious these birds could get. Meanwhile the farmer and his buddies thought watching me running across the farm from this angry rooster was funny as hell. It probably was hilarious to watch, but it wasn't that much fun for me.

The experience came in handy because that wasn't the only time I got a job putting fresh eggs in a basket. I was about midway along my trip when I met a farmer in another small town. I had pulled off the road and was milking a beer at the local bar where I struck up a conversation with a local farmer. I mentioned to him something about coming from New York and having some big job waiting for me in California, and hw my parents were so worried about me whenever I set out on the road, and a lot of other bullshit. The further I went on the trip, the better I got at bullshitting about the entire purpose of the trip. Anyway, when I mentioned that I was looking for some day jobs to pay for gas and food, he offered me a job on his poultry farm putting the eggs in baskets. I said sure, this time knowing to be on the lookout for any roosters.

So, by a warm invitation, I followed him back to his place where he introduced me to his family. He had a lovely wife and teenage twin daughters, both of whom were cute and looked fit and tan from working on the farm. The family invited me to have dinner with them, so I gladly accepted. There was never a time I turned turn down free food along my journey. By the time evening fell, it was decided that it would be best if I didn't sleep in the house, since I was a complete stranger. I didn't mind; I was happy to have a good meal, work and a place to sleep. He took me out to his set up in the barn and showed me where he had two bunk beds set up. It wasn't bad at all. Most people think of barns and envision a shack of some kind, but barns used by professional farmers are pretty nice buildings—some even have living quarters built upstairs for workers. For me, I was content with the bunk bed set up.

The bunk bed was comfortable and welcoming, and he had given me a blanket, so I was lying there ready to go to sleep in this big old barn when I heard some noise in the darkness. It was about 11 or 11:30 P.M. and someone was in there. I was frozen in place. I couldn't imagine what or who it could be. Thoughts came rushing through my head a mile a minute. I wondered if the whole thing had been a set up to mess with a "city boy" like me and now I was being ambushed. I thought about other people who had been at the bar. Had any of them been suspicious? I couldn't remember.

I looked up into the darkness and saw a dim light approaching me. Before I could make out the figure I cleared my head and prepared to run. Then I saw the person in the light. It was one of the twin girls carrying a lantern and a couple of beers.

My relief consumed me, but I didn't want to show her I was a bit startled by the unexpected entry, so I sat up cheerfully and took the beer, which was another thing I never turned down along the way. She sat beside me and smiled as she cracked hers open and knocked it back. Her name was Kellie and she asked if I cared if she hung out with me for a while. Of course, I didn't! So, we drank the beers and she started getting a bit closer, and it wasn't too much longer before we started kissing. Next thing I know, she was taking off her pajama top and things were really heating up in that chilly barn. After about twenty minutes of being with this farm girl, she got dressed, kissed me good night, and left. I certainly had not expected to be hooking up with the farmer's daughter that night in a barn in the middle of nowhere.

A few hours later, at what had to be around 3 A.M., I heard noises again. This time I wasn't so sure it would be a pretty girl. I thought about her dad. What if he found her sneaking back in the house and figured out what had transpired? I was ready to run again when I looked around, and there she was, back for more. I figured what the hell? Her father hadn't come to kill me and if he did, I'd die a happy man. So, once again she peeled off her pajamas and we went at it for another twenty minutes. After we were finished, and she was putting her pajamas back on, she turned to me and said, "By the way, I'm not Kellie, I'm Jane."

She looked at me and giggled before taking off back to the house. "Holy crap," I said to myself, it was the other sister. I could not believe it. Talk about a fateful encounter. Nothing like that had ever happened to me before...or since.

When I woke up the next morning, thoughts of their father began flooding my brain again. It was all too good to be true. He could have easily found out and was waiting for me to get up. This guy would definitely kill me, no doubt about it—even if I told him they came to see me, he'd still kill me. He was a big guy and I was becoming more and more paranoid. I started moving quickly, getting my shoes on and heading for my car. I really wanted to get out of there. Then, just as I was only a few feet from the car, I heard him yell from behind me.

"Hey Jimmy, I wanna talk to you a minute." I froze in my tracks. This was it. My life flashed before my eyes, the Randi's, the orphanage, my grandmother, my brother, the Bellandis, the crew, and finally, his daughters. It had all come to this moment. I turned around and there he was, holding a damn pitchfork! I thought about jumping into the car, but he was too close and could have jabbed me with that thing and it would have been over.

He said to me, "Jimmy…I need you to help me feed the animals, let me get you a pitchfork."

My heart started beating again, and I can't even remember the flimsy excuse that fell out of my mouth, but I remember saying, "I've really got to hit the road, I'm sorry." And with that, he paid me cash and I was in my car, driving away from the farm.

As I drove past the farmhouse, I could see the twins sweeping the front porch smiling at me. I guess I smiled back, but who remembers? I was hurriedly on my way back to Route 66 and with good reason.

Even ten miles away, I was still scared that they would tell him, and he would get every farmer in the area and come after me. My mind was racing, and I started thinking they might put up a roadblock to stop me. I couldn't stop imagining all the ways they were going to hunt me down and kill me—this angry mob of farmers that I was sure were now after me. I was literally scared to death. Fueled by anxiety and heart palpitations, I kept on driving for about five hours before I stopped in another town. I never saw that farmer or his lovely daughters again.

It took me a few months to get to Phoenix. I had stopped in so many places along the way I couldn't even remember them all. But the road trip was a hell of a lot of fun, and something I needed badly. I had to leave New York and put all of the many bad memories I had accumulated behind me. I also needed to change my life—as I mentioned earlier, I knew something better was going to happen to me. My supposition was that things would drastically improve when I arrived in Phoenix.

Getting to Phoenix

Chapter 10

On the final leg of my journey, I made my way from Route 66 to I-10 and which took me straight into Phoenix. Since there was nothing even close to GPS at the time and only maps and landmarks, I followed my aunt's directions to her house.

Aunt Rose was the older sister from my grandmother's home; Jeanette was the one who used to babysit for my brother and me and lived with us at our grandmother's place. I didn't know Rose very well and I hadn't seen her in years, but she had agreed to let me stay there with her. When I arrived, she was in the middle of making dinner. It's hard to say whether or not she was happy to see me in the traditional sense of the meaning of happy. She smiled, welcomed me and let me know that I could stay for two weeks. My family was never known for showing much warmth. She quickly made it a point to tell me I needed to find a job so I could then get a place of my own. Glad to see you too Aunt Rose, I thought, but I just smiled and agreed.

I now had a roof over my head and a place to stay. Quite honestly, I missed being on the road, but I knew that my voyage could not last forever. It wasn't long, perhaps an hour, before Aunt Rose suggested that I start my job hunt at the nearby Crisstown Mall, a popular place for shopping at that time. It had a variety of stores, some of which Rose told me had small signs in the window that said they were hiring. So, I got into my MGB, let down the convertible top (I loved parking it with the convertible top down) and drove the short distance to the nearby mall. I walked into the place and strolled around for a while. This mall was quite large and impressive. After maybe forty minutes, during which I did not see any help wanted signs, I decided to

188

sit down and rest. I found a number of empty chairs in what turned out to be a women's shoe store. So, I took a seat. As I looked around, I saw a middle-aged man, who looked a little like a white version of Sammy Davis Jr., waiting on a customer. He looked a little out of place in this mall in Phoenix. I was pretty sure he was a New Yorker. When he finished talking to the customer, he strolled over to me, wondering what the hell I was doing there.

With a bit of an attitude, he asked me, "Can I help you?" I understood where he was coming from, seeing a young man clearly sitting by himself in a women's shoe store. His inquisition also immediately answered my question of where he from. As I had guessed, he was from New York. Over the years, I became quite adept at picking up different New York accents. I'd spent enough time in Brooklyn to know a Brooklyn accent (that's an easy one), I could also tell the folks from the Bronx and I had a pretty good idea if someone was from Westchester, which is the area just north of New York City. I also had a feeling he was Italian, Greek, or Jewish.

I began to chat with him and I told him I was looking for a job. He picked up on my upstate New York accent, smiled and said, "You're hired." It only paid about $2.98 an hour (which would only be equivalent to about $12.50 today), but it was a start. Then I told him about coming from Syracuse and he said he was from White Plains (in Westchester). I knew it! He was probably about twenty years older than I was, but we had a New York connection.

After talking about New York for a while, I shook his hand, told him I'd see him the next day and left the mall to head back to my aunt's house. She must have gone out because there was nobody there when I returned, so I flipped on the television set and was sitting on the couch watching TV when she got home.

Clearly, she was surprised to see me.

"I thought you went off looking for a job," she said.

"I did," I replied.

"Well you're back pretty quickly. You're not going to find a job if you only look for an hour," she popped back with disapproval.

"I got a job."

"Where'd you get a job?" she asked with a tone of disbelief.

"At a women's shoe store in Crisstown Mall," and I told her the name of the store.

"I know that store, I shop there. How'd you get a job there so fast?"

"I know the owner," I said over the sound from the television.

I don't think she believed me, but that ended the conversation. The following day I started work, and guess who stopped by the store? Sweet Aunt Rose. Not only was Aunt Rose surprised, but she began to respect me a little more—after all, she figured now she could get a discount on shoes.

That was the start of my career in the shoe business. I never realized how much confidence I had gained over the years. As a kid, I liked to make people laugh, then as I got older I learned how to schmooze while hanging with the crew. On my cross-country trip, I also saw how easy it was to make friends with strangers wherever I went. All of those experiences culminated into the perfect training to become a salesman. It doesn't matter what you're selling. As long as you can win people over and they like and trust you, you are successful. In this case, it was selling ladies shoes; not a prestigious job, but simply a decent way to earn a few bucks. Pretty soon, it became a way for me to earn a lot of bucks. It didn't take long until I was the top salesman in the store.

I became friends with Pete, the guy from White Plains, who managed the store and hired me. He had been a trumpet player in a popular jazz band several years earlier. Pete and I would go out at night, chasing women and hanging out in clubs. I was no longer looking for food and trying to hustle anyone. I had a job, made an honest living, and settled into my own apartment in Scottsdale, just a few miles outside of Phoenix. I still had no loving family, but I felt a lot better about my life.

One small problem was that my MGB still had out of state license plates, which made me look like a visitor just passing through, and I really wanted to fit in. At that time people did not relocate very often, as they do today. In fact, the only outsiders in Scottsdale were snowbirds who came down from Calgary, Canada. Probably 100,000 people came down to Scottsdale every year to spend the winter, just like many New Yorkers who always spent the cold winter months down in Miami Beach.

One day before work, I decided to go to the Motor Vehicle Bureau and register the car so I could get Arizona plates. That was a huge mistake. Once I registered the car, the people who were supposed to be receiving the car payments, but could not find me out on Route 66, could now easily track me down…and they did. They weren't happy, and repossessed the car soon thereafter. I kind of knew that it could happen, but I made it too easy for them to find me by changing my license plates.

It wasn't a big issue for me because I had made some real changes in my life.

This time, for the first time in my life, I was earning enough money to go out and actually buy a new car. Suddenly things were falling into place. The kid who was out on the streets hustling for a buck and going from job to job had finally settled down. I switched jobs just once during my seven years in Arizona. With some help from Pete, I got into a top-of-the-line ladies shoe store in the area, a place called Diamonds in the Thomas Mall in Scottsdale, where I was earning nine percent in commissions. Pete said he would miss having me working for him, but he knew working at Diamonds was a much better deal for a salesman. I told him if he could get me into Diamonds, all his drinks would forever be on me. Sure enough, Pete came through, and we went out to celebrate…and as promised, the drinks were on me.

I had finally discovered that hustling was part of selling, only this time it was all strictly legal. Combining a little hustling into my sales approach worked very well—I was even winning salesman-of-the-year awards.

While working at Diamonds, one of the things I would do was start chatting it up with the customers. This was a high-end shoe store, so these ladies that came through the door had money. I knew that if they felt comfortable talking to me, after a while I could get them to buy at least one, if not several pairs of shoes.

For example, one day the wife of a well-known television personality came in the store. We started chatting as she browsed for shoes, but while we talked, she kept looking down a lot and I could tell that she didn't seem very happy. I asked her if she was feeling sad on that particular day. She told me her husband was always showing up in the newspapers in photos with some famous actress or model, and that she was getting sick of it. She confided that he wasn't paying much attention to her and she was becoming more and more certain that something was going on with at least one of the celebrities he kept posing with in the photos. She wasn't really so much sad as she was angry.

I told her that I was sorry she was having such a difficult time with him, but there might be a way that she could get back at him. This piqued her interest. "How can I get back at him?" she asked hesitantly.

"You could purchase a pair of the shoes you like in every possible color," I suggested. I added, "Just wait until he gets the bill."

She loved the idea, and by the time we were done she had found three pair of shoes she liked and bought all of them in seven different colors. She couldn't wait to see the look on his face when she showed him the 21 pairs of expensive shoes. I couldn't wait to see my commission check. It was a win for both of us. Sales at Diamonds was just a matter of giving these women a good reason to buy shoes, and I became pretty damn good at it.

The warm weather, the friends that I was making in Scottsdale, and the money I was now earning made life in Arizona a far cry from life in New York. I really didn't miss New York at all. I always knew that I had something better coming in my life, this was much better than anything so far, but I still believed there was more to come.

I should mention that there was one experience in Arizona that truly made me appreciate life. I remember driving my new car along a road just outside of Scottsdale. A lot of the area out there is desert, and that's pretty much what was on either side of this road…a lot of sand. As I was driving, I saw something in the road far ahead of me. I couldn't quite make out what it was, but it was moving toward me. It was huge and as it got closer, I began to think it was a tornado. So, there I was driving along and this tornado was bearing down on me. I had no idea what to do, so I just pulled off the road. At the moment I thought that this was it, this was as far as life was taking me. I braced myself for the impact. As it got closer, I could see it was much wider than a tornado, which is a narrow funnel shape. This was a massive wall of sand being whipped around like crazy.

Then, suddenly everything went dark and the car was pounded by a massive, moving, wall of sand. The force of it shook the car, but the car stayed right where it was. In a matter of a few minutes, it was all behind me. That was the scariest moment of my life. It probably blew past me in about five minutes, but it felt a lot longer. I got outside to look at the car. There was a ton of sand, and as I started brushing it away, I could also see that there were also a lot of scratches on my car. At that moment, I didn't really care very much; I was just happy to be alive and that my journey would continue.

I later learned that it was a sand storm, which is very common in dry, desert areas. It was frightening, but the sand storm did not scare me away from Arizona. I stayed for what turned out to be seven years before heading to Houston, Texas.

More Than Ever Imagined

Chapter 11

Before I explain the next chapter of my life, I must acknowledge that my time in Scottsdale, Arizona was terrific. I had left New York with nothing, and after too many years of struggling with no family, no love, and no money, I made a good life for myself. I used what I learned from the street wise university and became a top-notch salesman. It's amazing how much you can learn outside of the classroom if you keep your eyes and ears open.

If I had stayed in Scottsdale, my life would have been fine. I had a terrific apartment, plenty of friends, a nice car, and a steady paycheck. Sometimes you need to walk away from a life that is destroying you from the inside and get a fresh start.

It doesn't matter whether its three miles or three thousand miles away, like it was for me.

When I decided to move to Arizona, I was in a situation where I made a specific decision to take a chance on an even better life. I still believed there was something bigger and better on the horizon for me, just as I had when I was growing up; I just didn't know what was coming up next.

As it happened, a friend of mine (whom I had met in Phoenix) called me from Houston, Texas. He had moved there about a year earlier. He told me that I should come to Houston, and reminded me that I always said I was going to be somebody someday. He told me that there was a lot of money in Houston and a lot of great opportunities. So, I thought about it. I didn't know anyone else in Houston, nor had I even been there before. But I figured I'd give it a shot. I packed up my stuff, prayed for no more sand storms, and took the 17 hour, two-day drive to Houston.

This time, rather than sleeping in my car, I spent a night in a hotel. When I reached Houston, I went to visit my friend, who, unlike Aunt Rose, seemed genuinely happy to have me stay at his house for a while. As usual, it didn't take me long to find a job. This time it was at a window factory. I knew how to use my hands and I needed money if I was going to find my own place in Houston.

At first it was just another job; I didn't know anything about windows or doors except how to get through them when I was leaving some place like the orphanage or the Bellandi's house. But, as I worked there for a while, I got interested in windows and doors, and I learned as much as I could about them. Then, after about a year and a half I started to think about opening my own window company. The problem was that I was living hand-to-mouth off a weekly paycheck with no savings, no friends, and no family that I could call on to invest in a business. I had no collateral to interest any lenders and I had zero credit.

Then one day I was looking through the local newspaper and I noticed an ad for a marketing person to work for a contracting business. I figured marketing is pretty similar to selling, so I called the number and they told me to come in for an interview. I thought, why not? It turned out to be a very strange situation. I got to the office and met the secretary who told me that the owner, Kevin, wasn't in but we could meet later in the day.

Then came the strange part—she said, "Quite honestly, Jim, we're broke; we're ready to close the business down." I remember thinking, this doesn't sound very promising, why are they advertising for someone it they had no money? But I decided to meet the guy anyway. After all, I had nothing to lose.

I met the owner of the contracting business, Kevin, at a Denny's, and he was half an hour late. I could tell that he didn't like me from the minute we met. He was wearing a cowboy hat, cowboy boots, and tight jeans, and he spoke with a thick Texas accent.

There I was, this Yankee from New York, sitting across from him. We stared at each other for a few seconds and then he spoke, "I don't even know why we're meeting, I'm broke and if I hire you, I won't even be able to pay you. I haven't had a sale in eight weeks and I owe $15,000."

We continued to talk for a while and he told me a little about himself and his business situation. While I was listening, I started putting things together in my mind. I didn't have credit, but his father-in-law was the Vice President in a bank.

He had an office with one month's rent paid in full. He had a very nice secretary named Sandy on staff for another month. He had also established his business as a contractor for five years and had plenty of good ratings. The problem was that while he was clearly pretty good at what he did as a contractor, he didn't know how to run a business. While I was no expert, I saw some possibilities and started figuring out a plan.

I said, "Kevin, I want to work for you, but you don't have to pay me."

He looked at me and asked, "How the hell are you going to manage if I don't pay you?" I explained that I had managed on my own for years.

Then I explained my plan. "I want to make you an offer. Give me 49 percent of your company and that will mean I owe 49 percent of your debt...as soon as I put my name on your corporation, your corporation owes $7,500 and I owe $7,500."

He looked at me with knitted brows and blurted, "What?"

I continued, "Just listen to me Kevin, did you not just say you're ready to close the company? If you close the company, then you still owe $15,000 or you'll have to go bankrupt. You don't want to go through bankruptcy, do you?"

He squinted a little then said, "No, I don't want to go bankrupt."

Then I explained that if he closed the company and paid the $15,000, he'd still need to find a job somewhere. His wife, who was a head-hunter, would probably get him a job working on one of the oil rigs out in the Gulf of Mexico (which is where a lot of Texans worked at that time). I added that such a job sounded horrible. He agreed. He started paying more attention. Then I painted the picture for Kevin, explaining that if he gave me 49 percent of the company, which wasn't worth a dime, I would run the business. Then I asked him how much his gross net income had been per year. He said $250,000 for the business. I told him our first year we're going to gross $1.2 million, but I explained that we were only going to sell windows and doors because that's what I knew.

He thought about it for a few long seconds and said, "Okay, you're on." Now, I was going to be a 49 percent owner in a worthless company. I let him have 51 percent, so he would still be in charge and make the "big decisions". I didn't want him to think in the slightest that I was stealing his company, so he remained the majority owner.

The next day, we went to his lawyer's office and drew up all the papers. So, there I was in Texas for about two years and I owned a company, I had the rent paid for a month, I had a secretary, I had a phone, and it didn't cost me a penny. I wasn't making any pennies either, but remember, I did know how to sell.

In just a few months, I built up the company by working around the clock selling windows and doors. It was not easy starting a business. I was putting in twelve-hour days, seven days a week. We were putting everything we earned back into the business, until our accountant told us we should take some of the money out or we'd have to pay double taxes. So, we started taking money out and for two years we were each earning $100,000. Things were going very well until, out of nowhere, Kevin walked into my office and accused me of stealing his business.

This is why he had 51 percent, because I was NOT stealing his business, but remember, as I said earlier he wasn't very good at running a business. So, I asked him what the hell he was talking about.

206

He repeated that I had stolen his business and he wanted me out.

At first, I thought maybe he was kidding, but no, he was dead serious.

Another thing I had learned on the streets was "loyalty". Clearly, he had never been on the streets and knew nothing about such things. I was the one who took a huge chance on him, forming a partnership in a business that was $15,000 in the red and ready to shut down. I worked my ass off for two years so that this company was doing great and this was the thanks I got? Accusations of stealing his company? He had no concept of the fact that if I hadn't saved his company, he'd be working on some oil rig making a lot less than $100,000 a year. He just didn't understand.

I called my lawyer who had a copy of our signed agreement that stated that I owned 49 percent of the business. I asked him if he could really kick me out. However, since he owned 51 percent, my lawyer explained that he could kick me out of the office since he had more leverage than I did, but I was still entitled to my 49 percent of the money.

Kevin sued me, and I sued him back. Another thing about life on the streets was that I never had to deal with lawyers and lawsuits. People don't sue other people who have nothing, and at that time, I had nothing. This time, however, I had money in the company—49 percent to be exact.

Two lawsuits later, I walked away with a lot of money, it would be considered a fortune today. So, now I had enough to take $50,000 for myself for living expenses, and $200,000 to open my own business, and that's just what I did.

The problem was that I went through the $50,000 in about nine months, and I knew that if I started spending the $200,000 that was for business capital, I'd have nothing left to start a business and keep it going. So, I was essentially out of money again. One thing I can say for living in the United States is that if you need a job, you can always find one someplace. It may not be a good paying job, it may not support a family, but there's always a job if you really want one—a job that can put clothes on your back and food in your stomach. Anyone who says they cannot find some sort of job isn't really trying.

I got a job painting houses. I worked at night and ran the business by day. I didn't want anyone working for me to find out that I personally had no money, so I took painting jobs outside of the Houston area. How would that look for people to know the boss was broke? So, there I was, after two years of making over $100,000 a year, broke again. For a short time, I was working about 14 hours a day and raising a five year old son.

The first year of running my own business, I made nothing, which isn't uncommon for a new business owner. I had to pour whatever money the company made back into keeping it going. There were many nights I tossed and turned, sometimes never sleeping, but always worried about the business. Could I make it work, or should I just go back to Arizona and sell shoes? I had never grown a business all by myself, so this was new to me.

It didn't get too much better over the next few years. The one thing that kept me going was I knew this was better than being out on the streets with no job and no money. Starting up a business and keeping it going was easier than trying to get food every day on the streets as a 14-year-old kid.

After ten long years, the business took off. It was the early 1990s and in my tenth year of business I made a million dollars. I had always said something great was going to happen and it did. From that time forward the business has grown and grown into one of the largest window company in the entire state of Texas.

I tell this story not to brag, but to inspire others. The entire point being that I made it from having less than nothing, being hungry, and living on the streets, to being very successful. That doesn't mean it's about the money, it also means that I went from feeling bad about myself and my life to feeling great about myself and my life. I got married and had a family as well. I could have stayed in Arizona and sold shoes for years and I would have been just fine. Why? Because I was finally happy with life. I felt good about having overcome the pain I felt in New York from not having a family that I could actually call my real family. Yet, I had built a life for myself with a nice home, a nice car, and many friends; plus, I still had a good attitude about life. That was something that regardless of any situation on any given day, I never lost.

Life isn't all about making money. In fact, even before reaching Arizona, one of the greatest memories of my life was taking that cross-country trip along Route 66, and at that point I was still broke. It was great for me, because I was free from the pain that had kept me running away and searching for something I could not, at that time in my life, seem to find. That search for my own happiness, which I never doubted existed, is what continued to push me into situations where I could find opportunity.

Why am I Telling You This?

Chapter 12

When my brother graduated high school, he left the Bellandi family with a scholarship to attend Loyola University in Baltimore. He had even accomplished this in less time than it takes the average student to graduate from high school. He was well beyond average. I may have been extremely street smart, but my brother was the epitome of intelligence. He was someone whose intellect ran deep, not only in his studies but in the manner with which he carried himself. After doing so extremely well in school and graduating from college early, he continued his studies in seminal school to become a priest.

We spoke on occasion, perhaps two or three times a year. Somewhere in the conversation, he always had a way of making me feel inferior. It was a defense mechanism he had developed in all of his time being trapped in the life we were dealt. I understand that we both handled it different ways, and we both had to do what we had to do to survive—but it didn't make his words any less stinging. He was good with his words and he knew how to use them. He knew which buttons to push. It was true that I did not finish high school, nor did I go to college as he did, but I didn't need him to make me feel bad about myself—I had low self-esteem as it was and I had managed to overcome it on my own. I also learned to conceal my self-esteem issues much better than he did. I didn't take it out on others by making them feel intellectually inferior, or inferior in any way to me or anything like that. I learned how to smile and keep my focus on the better days I knew would come —that intrinsic belief made my optimism outweigh any of my self-doubt or the inevitable negative feelings that occur when anxiety would hit me or when I would feel the weight of the reality of my situation crashing down on me. I never allowed it to actually crash. That key difference alone made a huge impact in the differences in how our lives evolved. I could see that a crash was coming, but I didn't feel it was inevitable and I didn't feel helpless. I found a way out of it. I found a way to push through it somehow—even if it meant going really far away.

My brother thought I was a thug because the most recent visual memories he had of me were based off of when I was hanging out with a bad crowd (the crew), but I didn't care. I remembered that we had saved his ass a few times, us thugs, and for that, I was proud. I had a thick skin and let things bounce off me, at least that was how I got by, not letting what people would do or say stop me from going about my life. He hadn't seen me in years and he didn't know about all of the other things I had accomplished without the crew. He was much more absorbent of everything. We were polar opposites like that—everything ricocheted right off of me and everything sunk into him. He was a sponge for emotion, letting all of the negativity he had experienced absorb into him. He was also constantly harboring the self-doubt that comes with being abandoned time and time again.

As we got older and continued to talk, it wasn't all horrible.

He didn't constantly barrage me with insults or anything like that. In fact, he started mentioning to me more and more about his desire to find our birth mother. At first when he brought it up I thought he had to be joking. I couldn't, for the life me, understand why he wanted to seek the main person who was the catalyst for the suffering through which we survived all throughout our youth. We had totally opposite ideas regarding our birth mother. He wanted to find her and know where he came from, but not in the sense of a place. He wanted to know who he was deep down somewhere—a place where you can only truly know yourself.

He sought that from her instead of finding it within himself. He never would allow himself to believe that we very likely came from "bad stock".

I found this to be odd, since he had met our father and knew our grandparents. Our birth mother had married our horrible father and abandoned us. That was what we knew and that was how it was. Clearly, we were not from nobility, or anything even close. No one ever came knocking at either one of our doors to inform us that our entire childhood had been a dreadful mistake and we had inherited a Medici palace that was waiting for us in Rome. I don't know what he thought he would find by searching for her. If he expected blue blood to be running through our veins, I hated to tell him to prepare for disappointment. I couldn't understand it. I did not want to be any part of it; I thought it was a bad idea. I honestly didn't care where we came from. We did not have a loving family and that was not going to change.

I tried so hard to talk him out of worrying about where we came from and who our mother was.

I had conversations with him during which I'd ask him things like, "So what are you going to do when you meet her?" or "What do you expect her to be like?"

They were rhetorical questions. I wanted him, with all of his intelligence, to realize that she didn't give a damn, and if she did, she would have found us a long time ago. It was one thing if a mother was pushed at a young age to give up one kid for adoption because of the times and the pressures of society, but there were two of us! I didn't see how he could think that somewhere deep down she cared because I knew if she did care, she would have said something a long time ago. Hell, she could have gone to Unsolved Mysteries and had the whole country help hunt us down for her. But none of that happened.

I truly wanted some of my optimism to rub off on him. It didn't matter to me that we handled things so differently; he was my brother and I had always protected him in one way or another. Now I found myself in adulthood trying to protect him from letting the truths of our birth mother's life hurt him, just as I always had. I couldn't imagine how cold the remainder of his upbringing with the Bellandis was, but I had a feeling that it had somehow developed this unbreakable desire to find his real mother, at least to him. As far as I was concerned our birth mother wasn't our real mother. Regardless of who I may have felt our real mother was, I knew that he just couldn't feel the same way that I did about it.

So, my brother, then living in Washington D.C. as a priest and one of the founders of an orphan's foundation that raised money for kids like us, tracked down our birth mother. I don't know how he did it, or what type of resources and hunting it took, but after several years—and long before internet searches existed —he found her. She was all the way across the country, living somewhere near San Diego. He called me and asked if I would come with him.

I couldn't do it. I had to tell him no. I had no desire to meet her, to see her, to try and decipher her behavior and figure out if there was "good stock" hidden somewhere in her soul.

It wasn't worth the time or any emotional pain it might cause me. I didn't see what positives would come out of the situation. Never had I ever wavered in my desire to have a good day, regardless of what it took. Some would call that selfish, but it was self-preservation and self-love. Why would I deliberately seek to be hurt? I knew that finding her would only hurt.

Frankie had to make the trip across the country to meet our birth mother by himself. We were both in our forties at this point in our lives. I don't know what he was looking for, but I remember someone once having said to me, "You don't need to be mothered at forty." That person was right—the years of mothering, watching out for us and raising us with love were long behind us. As far as I was concerned there was nothing to be gained by following a trail that would inevitably lead to more heartache.

I mulled his reasoning over and over in my head. I wanted to understand him even if I didn't agree with the reasons he had thought out and presented for his decision to see her. Perhaps my brother thought that she would be wealthy or famous, and would welcome him with open arms. There was a chance, with all his seminary training and his ability to think deeply, that he contemplated the possibility that she would ask for forgiveness, or that something remarkable would happen that would somehow help atone for her abandonment of her children. That was not the case.

When he returned from his trip, he called me to describe what he had seen. He told me that she was living in a tiny trailer in some dilapidated trailer park. I remember that he described seeing an Alcoholics Anonymous certificate on the wall, yet noted that she still smelled of gin. The furniture was all old and dusty, and the interior looked just as bad as the exterior. From his account, she wasn't thrilled to see him. She greeted and hosted him like a stranger of no relation.

None of what he told me was a surprise, but I just told him that I was truly sorry it turned out that way, and I was—for him. I could feel it when I heard his voice, both before and after his visit, that he was truly seeking something from finding her and meeting her. He seemed to resent me just as much as her for all of the disappointment. He didn't respect me, he had never respected me, and meeting our birth mother couldn't make him respect me anymore.

Three days later, my brother climbed to the top of the eleven story building in which he worked, and jumped from the roof.

His immediate superior called to tell me.

I wish I was able to have talked him out of visiting her, or had realized how much pain he was in. I wished I had a chance to talk him out of what he did.

We came from the same parents and the same background. There were times when I wished I had never been born, but I always kept going forward. For some reason, he could not.

It's all about how you look at life. As I mentioned several times throughout my story, no matter how bad things got, I kept telling myself something good was going to happen to me. I never knew what it would be, but I knew life would get better. My brother did not share that belief. Like me, he wanted a loving family.

But neither of us could have that. I didn't let that stop me. He did.

In remembrance of my brother I wrote this book —telling my story.

For years I lied to people about my story. I told them I came from a good family, went to college, had lots of important friends, and so forth. I was ashamed of my background. As I got older, I began to realize how many other people, even wealthy and successful people, had their own problems and predicaments, so I stopped telling stories about my upbringing to embellish my life.

Someone once invited me to sit on a group of very successful people from homes with both parents, who were talking about their lives, telling their stories and being very candid. I listened and learned. This was before I became successful in business. It was then that I realized that even people with a lot of money had stories that were painful like mine. From that moment forward, I realized that I had nothing to be ashamed of;

I had overcome a lot and was (at that time) building my own business.

I tell my story now because I want people to understand that if I could make it to where I am today, anyone can succeed.

Again, it's not about making money. Instead it is about the reality that you can wallow in your sadness or you can keep looking for something better in life. That's why I kept running away—I always wanted to see what else was out there.

I had plenty of chances to give up on myself, like when I was in school being judged by the kids, and even by the parents. People saw me on the streets and hurried to get away from me. There were times that I was homeless and filthy, but still willing to work for a day's pay. People looked down on me. I could not control what they thought about me, nor could not control the fact that I was abandoned as a baby at a hospital or that my grandmother took me from the only loving family I ever knew (the Grandes) and placed me in an orphanage. I cannot change the fact that I still feel sadness during the holidays because I remember how I used to feel when other people gather with their families and I had no family to visit on Thanksgiving or Christmas.

For me the turning point came when I left New York and took my cross-country journey. I had freedom and that was what I needed. In Arizona I found the better life I was seeking. Then, in Houston I worked very hard to start a business and was successful. What will your turning point look like? Maybe it will be changing jobs, moving to a new place, going to a different school, leaving a bad relationship, finding new people to hang out with, standing up for yourself or working hard at whatever you love to do—starting a business, becoming a teacher, an athlete, a doctor or anything else you are passionate about. There are things in life that you cannot control, but there are also many things that you can take control of.

I hope this book will inspire others—remember, as I mentioned before—if I could make it, from my background, anyone can make it, especially if you never d-oubt that something better will happen in your life.